Meeting Jesus:
Face-to-Face with God

The Japanese calligraphy on the front cover and throughout this book is an artistic representation brushed by Yoshihiro Ishida of the Japanese character, *kami*, meaning god. The more complex character, *kami*, is a combination of two simpler characters meaning "to show" and "to speak." In other words, the Japanese word for god, *kami*, implies that **God is a "show and tell" God**, that he reveals himself through both words and concrete actions. This is consistent with how God is described in the opening verses of the historical account of Jesus' adult life written by John—one of his closest followers. These verses read as follows:

> *In the beginning the Word already existed.* The Word was with God, and the Word was God. He existed in the beginning with God. God created everything through him, and nothing was created except through him. The Word gave life to everything that was created, and his life brought light to everyone. The light shines in the darkness and the darkness can never extinguish it . . . .
>
> *So the Word became human and made his home among us.* He was full of unfailing love and faithfulness. And we have seen his glory, the glory of the Father's one and only Son.
>
> John 1:1-5,14 NLT

In these verses, Jesus is referred to as the "Word." As such, Jesus existed before the world began. He created everything and gave life to all that lives. Very directly, this passage tells us that Jesus was not only with God when all these things occurred, but was, in fact, God himself. Finally, these verses reveal that this same Creator and Life Giver became a human being and entered human history—that person being Jesus.

The GodMan Series and Collection

So then, **Jesus is both God and Man**. That is why the Bible studies in this book are part of *The GodMan Series*. Iwa produces a range of ministry resources. *The GodMan Series* is a subcategory of **The GodMan Collection** which includes Bible studies and other resources specifically designed to broaden and deepen one's understanding and relationship with Jesus.

Meeting Jesus:

Face-to-Face with God

Stanley Kenji Inouye
Heather Nagaki Inouye

Cover Art
Yoshihiro Ishida

Cover Design and Layout
Stanley Kenji Inouye

Published by Iwa, Inc.
P.O. Box 3796
Gardena, CA 90247-7496

First Edition

ISBN-13: 978-0-9835238-3-3

Acknowledgements

This book is the result of team effort. Although Stan and Heather focused most on the stories, everything else—concept design, interactive content development, cover art, editing, proofing, layout, production, promotion and distribution—involved the collaboration of the staff, board members and volunteers of **Iwa**, especially Iwa's Executive Director, **Cyril Nishimoto**, Office Administrator, **Ellen Fukuyama** and Stan's wife, **Janie**.

The **primary purpose of Iwa** is to develop training, tools and other ministry resources that enable Christians and churches to more effectively relate the Gospel of Jesus Christ to Japanese Americans and others of Asian ancestry here in the United States. In addition, what Iwa produces may well be of significant benefit to those of many other cultural backgrounds in America and elsewhere in the world.

We extend special thanks to the leadership of **Cerritos Baptist Church, Gardena Valley Baptist Church, First Presbyterian Church, Altadena** and **Valley Springs Presbyterian Church** in Roseville for their invaluable contribution by helping to beta test *Meeting Jesus: Face-to-Face with God* in small groups at their churches.

Table of Contents

Introduction

Back in the 1990's, a lot of Christians, especially youth, were running around wearing colorful bracelets with the letters WWJD on them. These bracelets spawned a proliferation of other body ornaments, key chains, bookmarks, bumper stickers and you name it with those same letters emblazoned upon them. Do you remember what those letters stood for? Depending upon your age, maybe you do or maybe you don't. They stood for "What would Jesus do?" Great question. It would have been wonderful if all those wearing those bracelets actually did do what Jesus would do, but my question is "How many of them accurately predicted what Jesus would do in a given situation, and then actually went and did it?"

My guess is that few of them knew enough about the historical Jesus as recorded in the Bible—who he was and what he actually did two thousand years ago—to be able to come up with any sort of an accurate prediction. They probably conjured up their own idea of what a perfect human being would be like or shaped an imaginary Jesus based upon a conglomeration of fragmentary impressions gleaned from childhood Sunday school lessons, Christmas plays, Easter pageants, random sermons, and a variety of Jesus movies to come up with what they thought Jesus would do in whatever situation they were facing.

Why do I think this way? I was one of them. Way before the WWJD movement was even popular, I believed myself to be a Christian by following this same approach to life and pleasing God. I was a member of a family whose Christian roots went back for generations, and I grew up active in church. Later in life, I prayed to accept Jesus into my life as my personal Savior and Lord. I studied the Bible and tried to apply its principles to every area of my life. I went into full-time Christian work and to seminary. I taught classes at that same seminary, spoke at conferences and retreats across the country, and was a ministry consultant to Christian denominations, churches and organizations for many years. Yet, it wasn't until I began working on *Meeting Jesus: Face-to-Face with God* that the full reality of Jesus being a whole, integrated person became true for me—someone I could relate to and who wanted and could relate to me—person-to-person—in the present—right now!

Before this, I believed in Jesus and studied a lot about him in the Bible. I was sure that Jesus' Spirit entered my life when I put my trust in him as my Savior and Lord. I had experienced the work of his Holy Spirit in my life, empowering me to do what I could not do on my own. He had transformed me in ways that I trust helped others and furthered God's will and work in the world. But, did I have a very clear idea of the kind of person I eventually would become as Jesus gradually transformed me into his likeness throughout my life? Did I have a concrete sense of what it meant to have, inside my body, the very same Spirit that inhabited the body of Jesus a couple of thousand years ago? Did I understand what he would do and how he would go about relating with others around me as I went about my daily life if his Spirit in me was free to do so?

No I didn't, because my prior image of Jesus was fragmentary—made up of historical, theological, philosophical and speculative bits of information and insight that were randomly collected over the years. I did not fully picture him as a complete and complex person who not only lived in history, but was alive and well in me—thinking, feeling, reacting, responding and wanting to do amazing things in and through me if I let him.

I collaborated to write this book with my daughter, Heather, together with the help and support of the staff, board and volunteers of Iwa, the ministry I had helped to start over thirty years ago. The primary purpose of Iwa is to provide whatever is needed that will enable Christians and churches to more effectively reach and disciple Japanese Americans and others of Asian ancestry for Christ. The catalyst that led to writing this series was the request of Japanese American pastors who had been relatively fruitful by implementing the Alpha course, but felt such a program would be more effective among Asian Americans if it was modified to better relate to them and meet their needs. While we were convinced that Jesus could and would meet the needs of anyone and everyone who put their trust in him, we also believed it would be much easier for Asian Americans to respond to him if they were introduced to Jesus in the same way he reached out to those in the Bible—ways specific to their circumstance and culture. So, we agreed to take on the challenge. However, I did not anticipate how the process of writing this book would dramatically change my relationship with Jesus and transform my life.

The Bible tells us that Jesus is the "visible likeness of the invisible God." If this is true, then all anyone needs to do in order to find out what the invisible God is like is to find out what Jesus was like. This book was written to help those who want to get to know God, but have little knowledge of Jesus as recorded in the Bible and in history, to do so. It is also for those who, like myself, know quite a bit about God and Jesus, but want to have a more personal relationship with God.

To accomplish this, we chose to focus our attention on six different instances in the Bible where Jesus met people for the first time, each with their own unique needs, and, as a result, not only did he meet their needs, he also filled each of their lives with a new sense of purpose and joy.

After doing our own Bible study, and historical and cultural research, we compared what we were learning with biblical commentaries to come up with as accurate an understanding we could of each of the selected first-time encounters Jesus had with people. Once we had collected all this information and insight, we began to integrate it into first-person stories—from an "I" perspective—as if each person who met Jesus was telling his or her own story.

It was amidst the writing of these re-imagined and expanded Bible-based stories that Jesus came alive to me like never before. Not only were we filling in the gaps of the sparse biblical accounts, but we were also filling in the gaps of my fragmentary understanding of who Jesus was as a whole, integrated person, and how and why he did certain things to meet the deepest needs and desires of the people he met. Yes, we had to take some risks to fill in-between the lines of Scripture, because there was often more than one plausible explanation as to why things happened the way they did based on our study and research. We had to choose what, in our opinion, was the most logical and supportable explanation in order to create a seamless story of each account. While some of the incidental details of each story may not be what actually happened, we are convinced that the overall portrayal of Jesus in these stories truly reflects not only who he was, but also who he is today—right now—because of his resurrection.

As we worked on one story after another, Jesus became more and more fully a person each of us could have a relationship with, someone we wanted to have a relationship with, someone we could fully trust, someone we would gladly invite to enter into the center of our lives. It became possible for us to project into each of our unique futures and see how the Jesus in us would develop our character by giving us his wisdom, his courage, his sensitivity and his love, eventually enabling us to become fully integrated and whole persons like him.

Since writing the Bible-based stories in this book, my own relationship with God through Jesus has never been more intimate and deeply personal. The invisible God is no longer a difficult-to-imagine, unpredictable force in my life. Now that I more fully realize that the Holy Spirit in me is just like the historical Jesus, he is no longer someone who is as difficult for me to relate to or predict as he was before. I now have a concrete understanding of who it is that entered my life when I first trusted in Jesus and the quality of person I will become, bit by bit, as I increasingly allow the Spirit of Jesus—the Holy Spirit—to shape me into a new, one-of-a-kind version of the "visible image of the invisible God."

All of us at Iwa, who partnered together to make *Meeting Jesus: Face-to-Face with God* available to you, pray that, as you read these pages, you will meet Jesus—for the first time or as never before—and be awestruck by who he is and the reality of the relationship he makes possible for you to have with him. And, as a result, your life will never be the same!   *-ski*

Reading Suggestions

Each chapter of this book is divided into two major parts.

The first major part includes *The Bible: "The truth, the whole truth, nothing but the truth!", The Story: "filling between the lines,"* and *Reflection Questions.*

This first major part starts by introducing you, the reader, to exactly what the Bible says about the first-time meeting Jesus had with the particular person in focus. It is essential that you realize what is biblical and what is imagined based upon what is believed to be sound biblical, cultural, historical and theological study and research but is nevertheless speculative. That is why each chapter starts with the exact words of the Bible for that particular encounter with Jesus under the section *The Bible: "The truth, the whole truth, nothing but the truth!"*

Then you will find our re-imagined and expanded story under the section *The Story: "filling between the lines."* It is based upon our study and research and written from the point of view of the person meeting Jesus for the first time. As was mentioned in the introduction to this book, in order to write these stories as if they were first person accounts, we had to make choices when there were several logical and supportable possibilities as to why things recorded in the Bible happened the way they did. We want you to be fully aware of what is actually Scripture and what is not.

Following the re-imagined Bible-based story, you are provided with *Reflection Questions,* a relatively comprehensive list of questions designed to help you ponder and digest what was revealed to you about Jesus and his impact upon others through the story. **It is not necessary for you to consider or answer every question on the list.** It is meant simply to be a helpful resource for you. Whatever you choose to do with the questions is up to you.

Originally, *Meeting Jesus: Face-to-Face with God* was written for small group Bible study. The list of questions were designed not only to encourage personal reflection but also to help facilitate group discussion about the Bible passage and the re-imagined story in focus. You may want to use the reflection questions in this way as well.

The second major part includes the sections *Personal Application Starter* and *Personal Application Questions*. If you are reading this book alone and you are ready to move on to explore what implications a particular encounter with Jesus you have just read has upon your life, you may want to skip the *Personal Application Starter* and immediately move on to the *Personal Application Questions*.

The *Personal Application Starter* is a summary of the re-imagined story and Bible passage covered in a particular chapter. These summaries were originally written to help individual group members to remember what they had heard in the group setting and, as a result, begin to realize, when alone, whatever implications there might be for change in their own lives. As with the *Reflection Questions*, the *Personal Application*

Questions that follow the *Personal Application Starter* are also quite comprehensive. **They too are provided simply as a resource that you may choose to use, not use, or use anyway you believe would be helpful**—individually or in a group context.

Our primary goal for writing this book was not for you to learn a lot of information about Jesus, but simply to introduce you to Jesus as an actual person who lived in history and is alive now in Spirit—through the Holy Spirit. Our desire is for you to realize that Jesus is someone that you can know and enter into an actual personal relationship with right now—today—and, simultaneously, establish an intimate relationship with the invisible God Jesus perfectly reflected at the very same time.

We hope and pray you will find your journey through this book meaningful and life-changing. Enjoy!

Chapter One

The Zacchaeus Encounter
Jesus Instills Self-worth and a Positive Identity

The Bible:

Luke 19:1-10

Jesus entered Jericho and was passing through. A man was there by the name of Zacchaeus; he was a chief tax collector and was wealthy. He wanted to see who Jesus was, but being a short man he could not, because of the crowd. So he ran ahead and climbed a sycamore-fig tree to see him, since Jesus was coming that way. When Jesus reached the spot, he looked up and said to him, "Zacchaeus, come down immediately. I must stay at your house today." So he came down at once and welcomed him gladly. All the people saw this and began to mutter, "He has gone to be the guest of a 'sinner.'" But Zacchaeus stood up and said to the Lord, "Look, Lord! Here and now I give half of my possessions to the poor, and if I have cheated anybody out of anything, I will pay back four times the amount." Jesus said to him, "Today salvation has come to this house, because this man, too, is a son of Abraham. For the Son of Man came to seek and to save what was lost."

The Story:

Hello. My name is Zacchaeus. I'm short, rich, Jewish, male, and a tax collector—the chief tax collector. I get other Jews to do the dirty work for me. My own people hate me because I work for the Romans, the ones in power around here. But I don't care because my own people were never very nice to me. Ever since I was a kid, they all looked down on me because I was so short.

I hated being short. I hated myself every day of my life. Nobody expected much of me, and I didn't either. I told myself, "Being short doesn't make you stupid, Stupid!" Because of it, I blamed my parents, God, and even myself for being what I had no power to change.

I also hated being born a Jew instead of a Roman. I tried to convince myself that being Jewish didn't automatically make you inferior. But I failed at that too. So, from a young age, I set out to prove everyone wrong, including me. And, I did what I set out to do. Or, so I thought.

I started off by creating my own opportunity. I looked around Jericho and noted the most successful Jews—the wealthiest and most powerful—were tax collectors. The Jewish community hated them, but still they had the most money and influence. That's because they could collect whatever they wanted as long as the Roman government got their share. If I had that kind of power and influence, people wouldn't dare look down on me. They would have to show me respect by being nice to me or I would raise their taxes. And, all this was not only allowed, but enforced by the Romans, otherwise it was impossible to get anyone to do this filthy job.

I considered everything, even the cost of being rejected even more, but I didn't care. I was numb. I manipulated, lied, and flattered my way into being hired as a tax collector. And eventually, I even became the chief tax collector—wealthy and powerful beyond my wildest dreams. And, you know, it didn't even bother me that I became rich at the expense of my own people. At last, nobody could say I would never amount to anything. I learned the system and made it work for me. I got everything I wanted—big house, servants, fine clothes, the best food, beautiful wife and children. This short, "stupid" Jewish guy was ordering people around. I sure showed them—inferior?—me?—hah! I was short, but a big shot! But underneath it all, I was lonely and paranoid. I didn't know whether those around me liked me, or merely what my money and power could do for them. I didn't trust or confide in anyone. Sometimes, I even wondered, "Do my wife and children really love me?"

The big Jewish family I grew up in was close and proud of our cultural heritage. Now, they didn't want anything to do with me. I broke my father's heart—in his eyes, I brought shame to myself, our entire family, and Jews everywhere. I consoled myself that I wasn't totally motivated by ambition and greed— that I wanted a better life for my children and to take care of my parents in their old age. But, whatever I gave my mother and father came right back.

Rich, but worthless. That's what my life was like. Then came Jesus and everything changed. Absolutely everything!

Here's what happened:

It was an ordinary day. I was going about my business, supervising my team of tax collectors, when, suddenly, a child of one of my servants came racing into the courtyard of our home yelling, "Jesus is coming!" Now, Jesus is a common name among my people, but the way the little boy announced the arrival of this Jesus could mean only one thing—Jesus of Nazareth was coming.

For some time, rumors about this Jesus had been flying around all over. And the rumors were growing more spectacular all the time. Some even believed him to be the Messiah, the long sought-after Savior who would come and deliver us from Roman oppression. But, not everyone believed this. Some accused him of being a religious heretic. Others felt he was a magician. Still others believed he was just crazy. But, no matter what people imagined him to be, he drew a crowd wherever he went. Nobody could deny the amazing things that happened whenever he was around. His arrival made everyone curious to see what would happen. They expected a great show and I was no different. I welcomed anything to escape my miserable existence for a moment.

But more than curious, I was eerily hopeful. For some time, I had been secretly pursuing my Jewish religious roots. I felt there just had to be something else, something deeper, some other purpose in life—power and wealth left me empty. So, I befriended some religious Jews by lowering their taxes and began probing them for more insight into Judaism than my early Jewish childhood afforded me. I especially wanted to hear more about the Messiah because of the buzz that this Jesus might be he. If he was the Messiah, and delivered us from the Romans, I guess I'd be out of a job. But, I wasn't worried. I had enough wealth for four lifetimes.

My eerie hope was built on what I learned about the Messiah—that he would not only free us from Roman rule, but would establish a new kingdom—a place of what we Jews call "shalom"—where everything is as it should be—a place of peace. I longed for peace—inner peace and outer peace. And, I yearned for purpose—purpose that would lead to love and trust rather than to distrust and isolation. My curiosity was piqued even more when I heard that a tax collector was one of Jesus' closest followers. Why was he willing to leave everything to follow Jesus? Did he find in Jesus what I was so desperately seeking?

As Jesus approached nearer with his mother, close friends and other followers, word spread like wildfire. The crowd around him grew ever larger, moving like a cloud across the sky. Joy and expectation filled the air. When the procession finally reached town, multitudes, shoulder to shoulder, lined the streets. People were even packed between buildings and peering from rooftops. As Jesus meandered along, the crowds, several layers thick, pressed forward trying to get a better look. They created a high impenetrable wall for those behind it who wanted to see, especially for those as short as me.

First, I ran ahead, then went back and forth behind the crowds and buildings trying to see until I finally spotted low branches on a sycamore-fig tree—I thought I could climb above the crowd and get, at least, a peek at Jesus. Maybe I could even get his attention and meet him in person. Loud second thoughts started to flood my mind—maybe I would get too much attention. Not only would Jesus notice me, but everyone in the crowd would notice me. Sure, I loved to be seen—in all my splendor and glory—surrounded by my entourage of bodyguards, but this was different. I would be humiliated if anyone saw me up a tree. But who cares—I really wanted to see Jesus. So up the tree I went.

It was a lot harder than I thought. It took a long time, but I was determined to get my short, overfed, well-dressed, middle-aged body up that tree. Twigs snapped beneath my feet and leaves floated down on top of someone's head. Whoever it was looked up and cried out, "It's Zacchaeus, the chief tax collector!" I had spent my entire adult life trying to impress on people that I was a man, however small, of power, wealth and dignity, and here I was up in a tree, dripping with sweat, torn robe, naked legs dangling from both sides of a flimsy tree limb.

Other heads turned and soon the crowd below was an ocean of scowling faces. The scorching air was now filled with jeers and laughter. There was nowhere for me to go. Insults were hurled at me like rocks at a frightened bird. Then another voice with a different tone emerged from the masses. Not one of harassment, but of calm acceptance. My focus had switched from scanning the horizon for Jesus to watching the stormy sea beneath me. I had lost track of Jesus, so I was surprised to discover him at the foot of my precarious perch.

Jesus looked up and said, "Zacchaeus, come down immediately. I must stay at your house today." I was astonished. Why did he say that? Why would Jesus need to stay at my house today—of all people? Normally, I was the one chasing people down and demanding what I wanted. Strangely, I wasn't offended—being ordered around that way. His words came across more like an invitation than an order—a gift. The warmth and affection behind his voice, though a man's, was like my mother's as she wiped tears from my fearful eyes when I was a child. I felt as if Jesus was offering me aid and comfort, protection from harm. Now I had to figure out how I was going to gracefully get down out of that tree. All of a sudden, I didn't care about power, wealth or appearances. All I cared about was getting down to be with Jesus.

When I landed at the bottom, I picked myself up and there I was standing face-to-face looking up at him. Close up, he was so ordinary looking. Yet, he mesmerized me! I was so utterly grateful he wanted to spend time with me—at my house—I hugged the man. Or, was he just a man? Anyway, I was so overjoyed, I didn't think twice. I then grabbed his arm and began guiding him through the huge crowd, navigating our way to my home.

I began to hear jealous muttering, "He has gone to be the guest of a 'sinner.'" Once again, I guess I should have been offended, but I wasn't. I was a sinner. When face-to-face with Jesus, all my self-justification for the nasty things I had done vanished. Compared to Jesus, I realized, everyone is a sinner. But, then it dawned on me. Their criticism was not aimed at me, but at Jesus for befriending me. What Jesus had done was divert the ridicule away from me and directed it towards himself. He was bearing what I deserved. He deserved none of it! Then I did get agitated. I wanted to lash back, but Jesus just calmly walked on.

Then, I sent one of my servants on ahead to let my household know that I was bringing home a special guest and that they were to prepare a feast in his honor. When we arrived, my house was filled with people bustling about making sure everything was set out for us. We spent the rest of the day reclining at the dining table, eating and drinking, in relaxed conversation. It was a wonderful time of getting to know Jesus and those who traveled with him. Jesus asked each of us in my household questions about ourselves. He was intently interested in each person, no matter whether young or old, master or servant. Nothing seemed too trivial to catch his attention. He was fascinated about every detail of our lives. We wanted to know more about him, but his focus was clearly on getting to know us.

We did learn about Jesus, but not so much from Jesus himself. We learned about him from those who traveled with him. They freely shared their stories with us. We found out about their lives, before and after they met Jesus. Their lives now were so full of purpose—lives filled with adventure and hope, growing wonderment as they faced each new day with Jesus. He surprised and amazed them at every turn. Obviously, the story most helpful to me was that of the tax collector who had left everything to follow Jesus.

It was not only their words that made such an impression, but it was who they were—as individuals and together. They were people on a journey together. They shared a purpose and a leader worthy of their sacrifice. Jesus was knitting them into the people belonging to a new kingdom. I could see that Jesus and his friends had the true riches I needed, and even though I had all the wealth and power, I was the real pauper. We were gathered in my home but it was clear that Jesus was the real host, honoring and serving everybody, including me.

I wanted to join Jesus and his followers so I could help bring about this new kingdom. Immediately, I knew what I had to do. I needed to right the wrong I had done, and become part of the solution rather than a major perpetrator of the problem. I rose from the table and announced, "Look, Lord! Here and now I give half of my possessions to the poor, and if I have cheated anybody out of anything, I will pay back four times the amount." Did that actually come out of my mouth? After a lifetime of getting all I could by any means necessary, I could hardly believe what I had said. But, I meant it. I truly did! And, as that realization swept over me, Jesus said, "Today salvation has come to this house, because this man, too, is a son of

Abraham. For the Son of Man came to seek and to save what was lost."

Jesus' pronouncement startled me. He declared that I was reinstated on that very day to the faith, identity and community I had lost—I was once again a "son of Abraham," a descendant of the very first Jew—a Jew, not by birthright, but by faith in God. And, it was to Abraham that God had promised that, through his descendants, all the nations of the world would be blessed. All those in my home were astounded that I was able to instantly redirect my life.

To say the least, Jesus changed my life. I have come to value myself more as Jesus saw value in me. Increasingly, I value others in the same way, too. I am far less paranoid about what others might think of me or do to me. I no longer obsess about proving myself to others or myself. I trust and love others much more freely. And, I have developed a whole new appreciation for the way God made me—short and Jewish. In fact, I am far more thankful for all of who God made me to be.

I was saved from myself, and plenty of people were saved from me as well—especially my family. And, just imagine how the people responded and how our entire community was impacted, economically, socially and spiritually, when I actually did give away half my wealth to the poor, and paid back those I had defrauded four times what I had cheated from them. What I have told you is only a small part of a story far bigger than my own. I am just so grateful that God has included me in what he is doing to bring healing and wholeness to one household after another.

Thank you for listening!

Reflection Questions:

- What did you learn about Jesus (his identity, personality, character, appearance, background, values and beliefs)?

- What did you learn about the way Jesus related to people?

- What risk did Zacchaeus take by climbing the tree? Why would he take such a risk?

- What did Zacchaeus hope to accomplish by catching a glimpse of Jesus? If he had only seen Jesus from afar but had not met him as he did, how do you think the story would have gone?

- Why would Jesus single out Zacchaeus as a person he wanted to spend significant personal time with? What risk did Jesus take by going home with him, and why did he take it?

- Do you think Jesus intentionally deflected attention and criticism away from Zacchaeus and onto himself? If so, why would he do that? If not, why not? How do you feel about what Jesus did? What does this say about the kind of person Jesus was?

- How did Zacchaeus undergo his amazing transformation? What do you think of the old versus the new Zacchaeus? Do you believe people can actually change like that? Why or why not?

- What do you think of Zacchaeus' decision to give away half of his wealth to the poor? And why did he choose to give it to the poor? What impact would this generous transfer of wealth have on his community?

- What do you think of Zacchaeus' decision to pay back those he cheated four times the amount? Wouldn't simple repayment with interest have been enough? What impact would this extreme act of justice and generosity have on his community?

- Why did Jesus call Zacchaeus "a son of Abraham"? How do you suppose Zacchaeus felt about being called "a son of Abraham"?

- What impact did what occurred in Zacchaeus' house have on others beyond his immediate household?
    - The gawkers outside looking in
    - His fellow tax collectors
    - The followers who were with Jesus
    - Zacchaeus' neighbors
    - Zacchaeus' friends and relatives

- Is Zacchaeus someone people today can relate to? Why or why not?

Personal Application Starter:

Zacchaeus was extremely short and Jewish. The Romans, the occupying power in the region, oppressed the Jews who lived there. And the Jews oppressed him all his life for being so short. Zacchaeus failed to see the justice in all of this, so he chose to turn the system in his favor. He became, after a lot of hard work, the chief tax collector for the Roman government. As a result, he became both rich and powerful on the backs of his fellow Jews. But his seeming success didn't satisfy him. He only became more lonely and unfulfilled. So, he secretly searched his Jewish religious roots for meaning and purpose in life. He especially probed those who helped him understand the Jewish faith for information about the Messiah, the Savior of the Jews. The reason he was so keenly interested in the Messiah was because many were saying that Jesus was that very person. The Messiah would deliver the Jews from all those who oppress them, including the Romans, and usher in a permanent state of peace and justice. Zacchaeus was not so much motivated by political peace and justice, as he was by a yearning for inner peace and relational equality. He was tired of being unfairly judged all his life.

Jesus was teaching and performing many miracles in the area. Huge crowds were following him wherever he went. One day, Jesus and his followers came to Zacchaeus' hometown. As the masses crowded the narrow streets to greet Jesus, Zacchaeus climbed a tree to see if he could get a glimpse of this supposed Savior. The reports he had heard about Jesus had convinced him enough that he might well be the Messiah that Zacchaeus was willing to risk the embarrassment of being discovered up in that tree. His fear was realized when someone recognized him and called out his name. What shocked Zacchaeus was that one of the voices that emerged from the crowd was that of Jesus.

Jesus told Zacchaeus to come down from the tree right away and take him home to stay for a while. By doing so, Jesus had diverted the ridicule from Zacchaeus to himself. First the crowds had jeered at Zacchaeus for being up in the tree. Now they were sneering at Jesus for going to stay at the house of a "sinner."

With the harassing crowd outside, Zacchaeus and his household were able to quietly spend some time with Jesus and his followers. Over the hours they spent together, Zacchaeus was able not only to hear Jesus teach about the coming Kingdom of God, but also to observe and experience the way Jesus and his followers related to one another. Although Jesus' followers were not perfect by any measure, Zacchaeus recognized that they were well on their way to becoming fully representative of the very kingdom Jesus taught about—a people of peace and fairness. He experienced nothing but respect and acceptance from Jesus and his followers. Zacchaeus became so convinced of the authenticity of what Jesus taught and the relationships that his followers demonstrated, that he wanted to become a Jesus follower, too—a person of peace and fairness. So Zacchaeus rose from the table and announced that he was going to give away half of his possessions to the poor, and, if he had cheated anyone of anything, he would repay them four times as much. To this Jesus proclaimed that salvation had come to Zacchaeus and his household that day—that he and his family had been restored to all the promises made to the Jews, that they would come true for them, too. Then Jesus said that what just happened to Zacchaeus and his household was a concrete example of what he, the Messiah, had come to do—"to seek and to save what was lost."

The repercussions of what happened that day in Zacchaeus' home were felt throughout the area. Not only had Zacchaeus changed the economic picture of his hometown, but he also transformed his relationships with the people and their opinion of Jesus—some even became followers of Jesus, too!

Personal Application Questions:

- What impact did Zacchaeus' story have on you, if any? Did it open your eyes or heart to anything new? What, if anything?

- Do you have some characteristic—physical, social, cultural, or otherwise—that you have felt you must overcome in order to be accepted or successful? If so, how have you dealt with it? If not, how have you treated or felt towards those who have such a characteristic?

- Have you struggled with a negative self-image or a lack of self-esteem? If so, how have you dealt with it? If not, how have you treated or felt towards those who have a negative self-image or a lack of self-esteem?

- Have you ever felt the need to compromise yourself in order to fit in or be accepted by others? If so, how did you feel about what you did, and where has it led you? If not, how have you treated or felt towards those who have made such a compromise?

- Have you ever discovered that whatever it was that you had worked so hard to achieve or attain, in the end, wasn't worth what it cost you, or wasn't as fulfilling as you expected it to be? If so, how have you coped with the situation? If not, how would you cope with it if it had happened to you?

- Have you ever sensed that God was "calling your name" in an attempt to get your attention? If so, how have you responded? If not, how would you respond if God did?

- How would you have felt if Jesus wanted to visit your home and spend time with you? If Jesus wanted to spend time with you now, how would you respond?

- How might you envision spending time with Jesus? What might you talk about with him? How do you imagine Jesus might respond to your questions or to the way you live?

- After meeting Jesus, Zacchaeus demonstrated a changed heart by announcing plans to do extreme acts of justice and generosity. If you became a follower of Jesus, how might he change your life and the lives of others around you?

Chapter Two

The Woman at the Well Encounter
Jesus Wipes Out Guilt and Shame

The Bible:

John 4:1-42

The Pharisees heard that Jesus was gaining and baptizing more disciples than John, although in fact it was not Jesus who baptized, but his disciples. When the Lord learned of this, he left Judea and went back once more to Galilee.

Now he had to go through Samaria. So he came to a town in Samaria called Sychar, near the plot of ground Jacob had given to his son Joseph. Jacob's well was there, and Jesus, tired as he was from the journey, sat down by the well. It was about the sixth hour.

When a Samaritan woman came to draw water, Jesus said to her, "Will you give me a drink?" (His disciples had gone into the town to buy food).

The Samaritan woman said to him, "You are a Jew and I am a Samaritan woman. How can you ask me for a drink?" (For Jews do not associate with Samaritans).

Jesus answered her, "If you knew the gift of God and who it is that asks you for a drink, you would have asked him and he would have given you living water."

"Sir," the woman said, "you have nothing to draw with and the well is deep. Where can you get this living water? Are you greater than our father Jacob, who gave us the well and drank from it himself, as did also his sons and his flocks and herds?"

Jesus answered, "Everyone who drinks this water will be thirsty again, but whoever drinks the water I give him will never thirst. Indeed, the water I give him will become in him a spring of water welling up to eternal life."

The woman said to him, "Sir, give me this water so that I won't get thirsty and have to keep coming here to draw water."

He told her, "Go, call your husband and come back."

"I have no husband," she replied.

Jesus said to her, "You are right when you say you have no husband. The fact is, you have had five husbands, and the man you now have is not your husband. What you have just said is quite true."

"Sir," the woman said, "I can see that you are a prophet. Our fathers worshiped on this mountain, but you Jews claim that the place where we must worship is in Jerusalem."

Jesus declared, "Believe me, woman, a time is coming when you will worship the Father neither on this mountain nor in Jerusalem. You Samaritans worship what you do not know; we worship what we do know, for salvation is from the Jews. Yet a time is coming and has now come when the true worshipers will worship the Father in spirit and truth, for they are the kind of worshipers the Father seeks. God is spirit, and his worshipers must worship in spirit and in truth."

The woman said, "I know that Messiah" (called Christ) "is coming. When he comes, he will explain everything to us."

Then Jesus declared, "I who speak to you am he."

Just then his disciples returned and were surprised to find him talking with a woman. But no one asked, "What do you want?" or "Why are you talking with her?"

Then, leaving her water jar, the woman went back to the town and said to the people, "Come, see a man who told me everything I ever did. Could this be the Christ?" They came out of the town and made their way toward him. Meanwhile his disciples urged him, "Rabbi, eat something."

But he said to them, "I have food to eat that you know nothing about."

Then his disciples said to each other, "Could someone have brought him food?" "My food," said Jesus, "is to do the will of him who sent me and to finish his work. Do you not say, 'Four months more and then the harvest?' I tell you, open your eyes and look at the fields! They are ripe for harvest. Even now the reaper draws his wages, even now he harvests the crop for eternal life, so that the sower and the reaper may be glad together. Thus the saying, 'One sows and another reaps' is true. I sent you to reap what you have not worked for. Others have done the hard work, and you have reaped the benefits of their labor."

Many of the Samaritans from that town believed in him because of the woman's testimony, "He told me everything I ever did." So when the Samaritans came to him, they urged him to stay with them, and he stayed two days. And because of his words many more became believers.

They said to the woman, "We no longer believe just because of what you said; now we have heard for ourselves, and know that this man really is the Savior of the world."

The Story:

You might have heard about the huge number of people in my hometown of Sychar who became believers in the Messiah. I know you must be wondering how so many Samaritans became followers of a Jew, in just a few days, especially because there is so much hatred and lack of trust between Jews and Samaritans. Well, let me tell you, it was a miracle, and I was in the middle of it.

It was a hot, dusty, nasty day when I met him. In other words, it was normal. Every day, I endured the midday heat to avoid the wagging tongues of the women who went down to the town well at dawn and dusk to draw water and gossip. I waited until they returned to their cool, dark, clay houses, before I came out into the glare of sunlight to do what I had to do to survive—fetch water. Every single day, I hated having to go out. As much as I tried to avoid people, still, somehow, there was almost always someone there to whisper behind my back. I would catch a stray word in the scorching wind—"shameful"—"sinner"—"whore!"

Why didn't I just leave this place, you ask? There is no place for me to go. You see, I'm a Samaritan. Way back in history, my non-Jewish ancestors married my Jewish ancestors, making me (and others like me) forever different from everyone else. We are our own mix of race, culture and religion. And because of this, we are shunned. We had to build our own towns to protect ourselves from prejudice.

On good days, we are a proud people. But, on bad days, which are more normal, we wake up and wish we were racially and culturally "pure"—free to move about and be treated like everyone else. Jews avoid us at all cost. They will even cross the

Jordan River east of our village to bypass us completely. Those Jews who rarely do come our way cross to the other side of the street when they see us coming so they can avoid being contaminated by us.

So, now you see why I couldn't just leave this horrid place. No place would welcome me. This is my prison.

When the time was right, my parents arranged a marriage for me to a young man from our village. It was all so normal. But, I soon found out he wasn't pleased with me. I caught him in bed with another woman. He was furious with me, and divorced me the next day. Men in my culture can do that. He can simply decide that he no longer wants to be married to me, hand me a written bill of divorce, and it is done. The marriage is over.

I was heartbroken and forever "spoiled" for marriage to another young man done in the usual way. So, my parents fixed me up with an old widower friend of theirs. But when I couldn't get pregnant—as if it was my fault—the old man threw me out!

In our culture, someone like me from a family without much money has few options to survive—either you beg, do the best you can to marry again or become a prostitute. I was too proud to beg and too religious to become a prostitute, so, I kept getting married. I kept hoping and praying that I would find the right man. But, each time, I had to compromise myself even more to get men to marry me, and then become ever more deceitful so I could get them to divorce me when I realized how much worse each successive marriage was. I might as well have been a prostitute. In my attempt to hold on to some shred of dignity by being married, I became the "laughing stock" of the women who gossiped around the well each day. I had invested all my hopes and dreams of happiness in men and marriage and after five failed marriages had come up empty—dry. I had been going to the wrong well in hopes of joy and fulfillment all these years. So, I finally gave up on marriage.

My family disowned me for the shame I had brought them. So without husband or family, I had no place to stay or call home. I had to do something to survive. That's why I chose to live with the last man without marrying him. We had an understanding. I did what he needed and wanted in exchange for food, clothes and shelter. Our relationship was a matter of convenience, not one of love and affection—not what I had yearned for all my life.

I was lonely, but relatively secure for the first time in years. I began seeking whatever might fill the vast emptiness within me and give me reason for living. One of the few people who would talk to me was a poor but kind merchant woman who sold me vegetables. She was old but smart—and very religious. Her faith gave her hope—hope that was built on the promise of the coming Messiah. She told me that when he came, he would not only explain the reason for all our suffering, but deliver us from all those who oppress us. Nothing changed on the outside, but a glimmer of hope was born and began to grow that someday things might be different. Then one day my hope became reality.

As the sun reached its highest point that day, I shuffled down the path to the well, wondering why God made me—unwanted trash. Then I saw a man sitting by the well as if he were waiting for someone. I stopped and wanted to go back—but the heat convinced me that it wasn't wise to make this trip twice in the same afternoon—ending up being heckled anyway. As I slowly approached, the man appeared to me to be a Jew. Once again, I wanted to draw back. But, then he turned his head and greeted me with a warm, welcoming smile. I doubted for a second that he could really be a Jew. Then, he motioned for me to come closer, and despite myself, I walked toward him.

He then asked me for a drink. I couldn't believe what I was hearing. I stood there stunned. First of all, as I said earlier, Jews have nothing to do with Samaritans. Second, whether Jews or Samaritans, men do not talk to women in public apart from their own mothers, wives or daughters. And, third, a Jew would never stoop to ask a Samaritan for help—certainly not to drink from a cup contaminated by Samaritan lips, and those of a woman at that!

I told him how astounded I was that he, a Jewish man, was asking me, a Samaritan woman, for a drink. He nodded thoughtfully. His reply startled me even more. He told me that, if I recognized who he was, I would be asking him for a drink of what he referred to as "the gift of God"and later identified as "living water."

I was so confused—one minute he asked me for water and in the next breath, he said that he would give me water. I knew every trail and ravine around here and there was no water that didn't come from this well that our forefather Jacob dug for us generations before. So, I told him that unless he was greater than Jacob and could make water out of thin air, he must be crazy. But then he went on to tell me that the water he would give me is not like the ordinary water Jacob gave us, but magic water that would quench our thirst forever and, on top of everything else, would bubble up from within us and give us eternal life. Another missed clue. So, still believing he was talking about drinking water rather than something spiritual, I asked him for some of this magic water so I wouldn't have to come back to the well any more.

But, he could see I wasn't getting what he was talking about so he abruptly changed the direction of our conversation by asking me to go get my husband and bring him back. Up went my defenses. But, perhaps he did assume I was married. After all, any respectable woman in my culture would be married at my age. I told him I didn't have a husband and said no more. I told him the truth. Right?

But then he really shocked me. He knew I wasn't married. In fact, he knew the exact details of my life—he told me about my five failed marriages and that the man I was living with was not my husband. He told me all this and yet complimented me for telling the truth when he could have condemned me for not telling him everything.

Wait! How did he know all this about me? Did he travel this way before and hear the gossip about me? Or did he get all this information from the same source as this magic water of his? I wanted to believe his knowledge of me came from the same place as the magic water, so I told him that he must be a prophet. And, if he was a prophet, I hoped he would also tell me why Jews hated Samaritans so much, and why we worshiped in different places. But, all he said was that there would come a time when it wouldn't matter where we worship, but only how we worship—in spirit and truth. He said that the "Father" seeks such true worshipers no matter whether they are Samaritans or Jews.

He just gave me two more clues to his identity. First, who would be able to refer to God in such a familiar way—as Father? Second, who else would talk about a time to come when the separation between Samaritans and Jews would no longer exist—that we would be united in our worship and equal in God's sight? When he said this, some of the clues started to come together in my mind and heart. Could he be more than a prophet? So I just blurted out, "I know that Messiah is coming. When he comes, he will explain everything to us." Then he stated plainly, "I am he."

Wow! That's hard to believe, especially when someone tells you right to your face. That means I was sitting there by the well, on a day like any other, having a little chat with the Messiah—the Savior of the world. Can you believe that? Part of me wanted to believe—even did believe, and yet the other part of me thought I'd be a fool to believe it. It all seemed too good to be true!

Just then, I heard a group of men approaching from behind us. I turned around and saw their surprised faces. I think they were shocked that he was talking to an unfamiliar woman in a public place. But, they didn't question or criticize him—or me for that matter. It was obvious that he was their leader and they respected whatever he did. He saw me squirm when the men arrived, so he allowed me to leave. So, I got out of there.

I was so excited that I forgot my water jar. I didn't fully realize what I was doing. I wasn't afraid of what people might think of me any longer or how they would treat me. I just knew I had to tell others about the man I had just met and all he said. Could he really be the Messiah?

It occurred to me as I was running back up the hill into town that he might have actually anticipated meeting me at the well that day and had sent his followers into town to get food so I wouldn't be intimidated by a crowd of men gathered at the well. Certainly, it didn't take all those men to buy lunch. I believe now that he knew that if there were a crowd at the well when I approached, I would have retreated and never come to the well until he and his followers were gone. But, that meant that he actually anticipated my coming to the well, wanted to meet me, and had sent his followers away so we could meet. In other words, he was waiting for me when I first saw him. Exactly how he knew all this I didn't understand. All I knew was he knew—another clue confirming to me who he must be.

When I finally got to the village gate, I begged everyone to come to the well with me so they too could meet the stranger who told me everything I had ever done. But, nobody was surprised. They must have thought, "What's so astounding about that? Everyone around here knows what kind of woman you are and all you have done!" But soon, it wasn't what I said that convinced them that the man I met at the well might be the Messiah; it was the change they saw in me. I was always so sad and edgy, avoiding anyone who came near. Now, I was approaching everyone with joy and hope. So it was now they who were urging me to return quickly with them so I could introduce them to this "might-well-be" Messiah. Others were not quite so convinced, but they came anyway. When we arrived at the well, he was still there with his followers. They appeared to be waiting to greet us.

When we arrived, they did greet us in a culturally customary manner, with kisses on both cheeks. But, what shocked us most was who greeted whom. These Jewish men were not only welcoming the men among us, but the women as well—as if we, both Jews and Samaritans, men and women, were equal. It was obvious that they were not entirely comfortable doing it—as if it were something they did everyday—but their leader, the man I hoped to be the Messiah, seemed to have coaxed them forward with the slight uplifting of his chin and a barely noticeable motion of his hand. But soon after we returned their awkward greeting with our own, the discomfort on both sides melted as we, little by little, began to talk more freely and eventually even pass water cups around to quench our thirst as we sat beneath the scorching sun.

We enjoyed being with one another so much, and learned so much from them, that we invited the man, along with his followers, to stay longer with us in our homes. We basked in his company for two more days. During that time, I asked the man about those very things that so intrigued and confused me when we had first met at the well—about the "gift of God" he also referred to as "living water," and about worshiping "in spirit and in truth." He patiently opened not only my mind to what he said, but my heart as well. I soon understood many things much better, like "living water" being a way of talking about the spiritual life that he could put within me that would empower me to live life now and into eternity in a way that would be totally fulfilling to me and pleasing to God. But, I still didn't fully grasp the meaning behind everything he said. However there came a time when I realized that I didn't have to fully understand everything to be able to put my trust in him as the Messiah. And, I was not the only one who came to believe in him during those two wonderful days. Many others also told me, "We no longer believe just because of what you said; now we know that this man really is the Savior of the world."

Oh, yes and by the way, the Jewish man I met at the well and soon discovered to be the Messiah has a name. His name is Jesus. Hope you meet him for yourself—soon!

Reflection Questions:

- What did this encounter with Jesus reveal about him that you already knew?

- Did you learn something new about Jesus (his identity, personality, character, appearance, background, values and beliefs) or about the way he related to people? If so, what did you learn?

- What had the woman been through that prepared her to meet Jesus?

- What changes did the woman go through in her perceptions of Jesus that finally led him to reveal himself to her as the Messiah? Why didn't Jesus come out and tell her who he was from the beginning?

- What is the "living water" Jesus referred to that he told the woman she would ask him for if she knew who he actually was? Did she eventually ask Jesus for and receive this "living water"?

- Was it necessary for Jesus to cause the woman to reveal her shameful past? Why did he do that? How did she feel about what he did? What do you think of her reaction?

- Jesus started off talking about things that were personal and private—living water and the woman's shameful past—and ended up addressing the much broader burning issue of religious, racial and cultural conflict between Jews and Samaritans. What connection was there, if any, between where they started and where they ended up?

- How do you feel about what Jesus said—that God actually seeks "true" worshipers regardless of where they come from or where they worship?

- On his way to Galilee through Samaria, Jesus stopped and initiated a conversation with just one woman and ended up spending a couple of days with a whole Samaritan community. Was this what Jesus planned all along, or was he just going with the flow? What do you think happened to the woman and the community after Jesus left?

- When the Samaritan woman put her faith in Jesus and believed that he was, in fact, the Messiah and Savior of the world, she did not have answers to all her questions. Why do you suppose she was able to believe that he was the Messiah before she had answers to all her questions? What do you think would have to happen before you could do as she did—believe that Jesus is the Savior?

- Is the Samaritan woman someone people today can relate to? Why or why not?

Personal Application Starter:

The Samaritan woman Jesus met at the well outside of her town was there at the hottest time of the day. Why? Because she wanted to avoid contact with as many people who knew her as was possible. Her past and present life was not one she was proud of. She had been married five times, and the man with whom she was living at that time was not her husband. She had compromised herself many times in order to gain the affection and temporary provision from the men in her life. She felt dirty, guilty and ashamed. She knew she had been the talk of the town at many gatherings by the well. Most of the women in her local village only went down to the well to draw their daily ration of water at dawn and dusk when the day was coolest. It was at those times, that all the local news was brought up to date. If she were to be there at those times, she knew the harassment she would receive. She learned this lesson the hard way, by being there at the wrong times.

She was also a member of a shunned minority of blended racial, ethnic and religious backgrounds—the Samaritans. She struggled with her biracial and bicultural background. Her town was an enclave of such people. In other words, she was shunned by people who themselves were a shunned people. Jesus was a member of the dominant culture, the Jews, and both his and her cultures were male-dominated. So, when she went to the well for water that day and discovered Jesus, a Jewish man, sitting there alone, the best she expected from him was to be ignored, but that is not how Jesus responded to her arrival. Rather than ignore, reject, ridicule or molest her, he talked to her and even asked her for help. Jesus asked her for a cup of water to quench his physical thirst.

Jesus soon turned their conversation away from his physical thirst to her spiritual thirst. He offered her "living water." In the process of answering her question about where he got this living water, Jesus revealed himself to be the "Messiah," the long sought-after Savior of Jew and Samaritan alike. Having given her proof of his claim by telling her the details of her shameful life, a miraculous transformation took place in her without her realizing it. No longer concerned about the ridicule and rejection of others, she rushed back to town to invite her fellow townspeople, men and women alike, to find out for themselves whether the man she had met at the well was indeed the Messiah.

Many from the town did follow her to the well to meet Jesus. Once they did, they asked Jesus to stay with them so they could get to know him better. Jesus and his followers stayed with the Samaritans two more days. As a result, many believed in Jesus for themselves, and they said, "We no longer believe just because of what you said; now we know that this man really is the Savior of the world."

Personal Application Questions:

- What impact did the Samaritan woman's story have on you, if any? Did it open your eyes or heart to anything new? What, if anything?

- Have you ever felt like this woman—ashamed of something about yourself, wanting to avoid the scrutiny of others? If so, how have you dealt with it? If not, how have you treated or felt towards shame-filled people like this woman?

- Have you ever felt like you're second-class because of your race, ethnicity, gender, social status, or economic class? If so, how have you dealt with it? If not, how have you treated or felt towards marginal people who have?

- If Jesus were waiting around to talk with you right now, how would you feel about that? And if you knew he accepted you despite whatever you've done in the past or whatever your race, ethnicity, gender, social status, or economic class, would it make a difference to you? If so, how would it?

- If Jesus offered you "living water," is it something you would want? What would you say to him?

- Jesus had to help the woman see her spiritual need for living water by bringing to her attention her shameful past. What might Jesus bring up to you that would be like the woman's five former husbands and the man she was living with who was not her husband?

- If God really seeks "true worshipers" as Jesus asserted, would God be seeking you? Do you worship God? If so, do you worship God in spirit and truth? If not, why not? Would you like to become a "true worshiper"?

- If you found out that Jesus was more than just an extraordinary human being, but one who could spiritually save the lives of all the people you care about, would you want to tell people about him? Whom would you tell?

- If Jesus were willing to spend a couple of days talking with the people you would consider being in your network of relationships—family, friends, co-workers, neighbors—how would you feel about that? What do you imagine you and the others would talk with him about?

- Jesus wiped away the shame and guilt of this woman who hid herself from the scrutiny of others, and gave her a new sense of acceptance, respect, dignity, and hope that transformed her into a bold sharer of her new-found faith and someone who positively impacted her entire community. If you became a follower of Jesus, how might he change your life and the lives of others around you?

Chapter Three

The Centurion Encounter
Jesus Transcends Culture and Status

The Bible:

Matthew 4:23-25

Jesus went throughout Galilee, teaching in their synagogues, preaching the good news of the kingdom, and healing every disease and sickness among the people. News about him spread all over Syria, and people brought to him all who were ill with various diseases, those suffering severe pain, the demon-possessed, those having seizures, and the paralyzed, and he healed them. Large crowds from Galilee, the Decapolis, Jerusalem, Judea and the region across the Jordan followed him.

Matthew 8:5-13

When Jesus had entered Capernaum, a centurion came to him, asking for help. "Lord," he said, "my servant lies at home paralyzed and in terrible suffering." Jesus said to him, "I will go and heal him." The centurion replied, "Lord, I do not deserve to have you come under my roof. But just say the word, and my servant will be healed. For I myself am a man under authority, with soldiers under me. I tell this one, 'Go,' and he goes; and that one, 'Come,' and he comes. I say to my servant, 'Do this,' and he does it."

When Jesus heard this, he was astonished and said to those following him, "I tell you the truth, I have not found anyone in Israel with such great faith. I say to you that many will come from the east and the west, and will take their places at the feast with Abraham, Isaac and Jacob in the kingdom of heaven. But the subjects of the kingdom will be thrown outside into the darkness, where there will be weeping and gnashing of teeth."

Then Jesus said to the centurion, "Go! It will be done just as you believed it would." And his servant was healed at that very hour.

Luke 7:1-10

When Jesus had finished saying all this in the hearing of the people, he entered Capernaum. There a centurion's servant, whom his master valued highly, was sick and about to die. The centurion heard of Jesus and sent some elders of the Jews to him, asking him to come and heal his servant. When they came to Jesus, they pleaded earnestly with him, "This man deserves to have you do this, because he loves our nation and has built our synagogue." So Jesus went with them. He was not far from the house when the centurion sent friends to say to him: "Lord, don't trouble yourself, for I do not deserve to have you come under my roof. That is why I did not even consider myself worthy to come to you. But say the word, and my servant will be healed. For I myself am a man under authority, with soldiers under me. I tell this one, 'Go,' and he goes; and that one,

'Come,' and he comes. I say to my servant, 'Do this,' and he does it."

When Jesus heard this, he was amazed at him, and turning to the crowd following him, he said, "I tell you, I have not found such great faith even in Israel." Then the men who had been sent returned to the house and found the servant well.

The Story:

When I received orders from Rome that I was to go and lead a troop of about 100 soldiers in the fishing town of Capernaum on the shores of the Sea of Galilee, I didn't know what to think. I would be under the authority of Herod Antipas, a powerful Jewish ruler whose family had received Roman citizenship as a result of outstanding service to the military campaigns of Pompey and Julius Caesar generations earlier. My men were to be a mixture of Romans and Jews. I didn't welcome the assignment because I knew nothing about Jews let alone leading them. But, I am a man under military authority, so I did what I was told to do.

When I arrived in Capernaum, I was like a duck out of water. I was in a strange land among strange people. Within my military compound, my soldiers and servants spoke Greek just as I did and related to one another as was customary to my upbringing. But, beyond the walls of this safe haven, the people spoke a very different language, lived according to a different culture, and believed in a different religion. I grew up believing in many gods. But, the Jews worship only one god—a god they fear so much they dare not even speak his name. How was I to lead my men without being embarrassed by my ignorance and insensitivity? The answer to my dilemma came in the form of a bilingual, very religious, old and trustworthy Jewish servant. He was indispensable in helping me adjust to my new duties as centurion and the mixture of men and cultures into which I was cast. He was not only my interpreter, but was also my cultural and spiritual guide.

Over time, I relied on my servant so much that I shared my deepest confidences with him. He proved to be a man of such integrity that I had full assurance that whatever I shared with him stayed with him. Being thrust into a new culture had an effect upon me that I didn't anticipate. I soon questioned all the basic assumptions of my own cultural and religious background. My servant was so patient and understanding that I poured out to him all my confusion over what was true and right. Whenever I had to make an important decision I made sure I consulted him. He was so full of insight and wisdom that I came to depend upon him as much or more than I did my own father as I grew up. I admired the man so much, I came to love and trust him like no other.

As I mentioned, my servant was also a deeply religious man. He not only faithfully observed the rites and rituals of his Jewish faith, but he had a level of relationship with his god that I had never before sensed in a man. My experience with the gods I worshiped was distant and impersonal. I prayed or offered sacrifice to them to appease them or get what I wanted from them. The god my servant worshiped was not someone who could be manipulated by such things but deserved worship for who he was, the God of creation, the God above all gods, the all-powerful and sovereign God. My servant would often recount to me the military history of the Jewish people and how, numerous times, his God would tell their leaders to reduce their forces or do other equally illogical things when facing overwhelming odds so that, if they obeyed and thus prevailed, they would know that it was God who delivered them and not anything they had done on their own power that saved them let alone led them to victory. It was this God that seemed to make such a difference in my servant's life so I began to want to know more and more about him. So, I asked my servant to teach me about his God and so he invited me to come with him to the synagogue each Sabbath to hear the Scriptures chanted and the prayers offered.

I understood little at first because both the language and rituals were foreign to me. But, over time, things became familiar and even comfortable. My servant and I would spend our Sabbath afternoons in relaxed conversation over a meal discussing the things that went on at the synagogue. He interpreted for me what was said and done so everything started to make sense. I even began to understand the language and culture of the Jewish people better as I gained a grasp of their religion. Others at the synagogue also embraced and helped me in my spiritual journey. Of course, they were at first defensive and suspicious when I first started coming to the synagogue. Who wouldn't question why a Roman centurion would come to a Jewish synagogue each Sabbath? But, over time and due to the good reputation of my servant, I was soon accepted as someone who was truly seeking to know and worship God.

The land and people were no longer strange to me. I began to feel at home in a new way. Capernaum became my spiritual home. I had grown a deep respect for the Jews and I envied them for the faith that united and enabled them to be such a resilient people. I learned of their hopes and dreams, that someday a Messiah, a Savior, would come and deliver them from all their oppressors and establish an ideal kingdom where justice and peace would prevail forever. As a result, I began to do what little I could to bring some degree of peace and justice to Capernaum as a result of my command as a centurion.

One of the things I did was to help build a new synagogue. The Jews had been heavily taxed by the Roman-backed government of Herod Antipas, and I was a part of it. So, the people had little money left to maintain their place of religious learning and worship, let alone make it a place worthy of their God. As my faith in God increased, my estimation of the synagogue's condition grew worse. God deserved grandeur and splendor, not a degenerating building with cracked walls and a leaky roof. So, with the astute advice of my servant, I was able to convince Herod Antipas that the people of Capernaum would cause far less trouble and be far more loyal to him if he would allow me to use some of my own money, whatever my soldiers wanted to give, and a small portion of tax revenues to help the Jews build a new synagogue. I told Herod it would make my job of keeping the peace so much easier and would actually save him money in the long run. Miraculously, he agreed. And so we were able to build a new synagogue. Praise be to God!

Spending time at the synagogue each Sabbath kept me in close touch with what was going on in the Jewish community. So, when my servant became paralyzed and was in great pain, I knew what I had to do as a last resort. I had tried all the usual means of medical help for my servant, both Jewish and Roman, but nothing worked. He just kept getting progressively worse and was actually on the verge of death. So, I finally decided to get in touch with a young Jewish itinerant preacher named Jesus who, reportedly, was healing all kinds of people of every kind of disease and disability. Because I was a Roman centurion, I felt that Jesus might not be inclined and might even be fearful to help my servant because of what he might think I might do to him and his followers. It seemed to me that I might have a better chance of convincing Jesus to come and help heal my servant if I asked some of the Jewish elders at the synagogue to go on my behalf. I had heard that, everywhere Jesus went, he taught in the synagogues and preached about the kingdom of

God. I was convinced Jesus would respond better to them than to me.

The elders were reluctant. They had different opinions about Jesus and what they had heard about him. They knew that Jesus had grown up not far from Capernaum in Nazareth, that he was the son of a carpenter named Joseph, and had no formal religious training. They were also aware that some of his closest followers were from Capernaum, including two sets of brothers who were partners in a fishing business. Rumors of how these brothers left their responsibilities to follow Jesus disturbed them. On top of that, everywhere Jesus went, he boldly stood up in the synagogues and interpreted the Scriptures as if he had the authority of God behind him. He went around telling people that the kingdom of God was beginning to be established right then and there. The elders did not believe anything they had experienced indicated that this was so unless Jesus, like so many others before him, presumed himself to be the Messiah, the Savior, and was referring to his growing following as evidence that the coming kingdom was now taking shape. I was convinced that this was true—that he was the Messiah. How could he speak as he did and do such miracles unless he was the Messiah? I think their judgment was clouded by the fact that Jesus grew up so close to Capernaum and they knew so many details about his upbringing but not all of it. To them, he was just the son of Joseph the carpenter from Nazareth. They didn't know about his miraculous birth or other facts surrounding his early childhood. However the news of all the people Jesus cured did impress the elders and, most of all, out of obligation to me for helping them build their new synagogue, they went reluctantly on my behalf to ask Jesus to help my servant. Just as

I sensed godliness in my servant, I sensed God in Jesus. I felt that, if anyone could heal my servant, it was Jesus.

A servant I had sent with the elders, returned with good news. He said, "Jesus is on his way!" A feeling of joy rose in my heart, and a new sense of hope lifted my spirits. When I asked him how the elders had convinced him to come, he said, "They pleaded with him. They told him you deserved to have him do this for you." Not certain I heard him right, I asked, "They told him what?" He repeated, "You deserved to have him do this for you." Unsure of what that meant, I asked, "Deserved? How did I deserve this?" He explained, "They said you built their synagogue . . . and . . . you love their nation." My heart sank. I hung my head and said "Yes, as true as that may be, those things still don't make me deserving of anything this great man of God might do for me." I was embarrassed that those I sent to represent me tried to appeal to Jesus based on my worthiness. I felt anything but worthy. And I had to let Jesus know.

So when I looked through the window of my paralyzed servant's bedroom, and saw Jesus and his followers approaching my house, I immediately told my friends, "Go quickly and tell Jesus that he need not come any further. Tell him I said I don't deserve to have him come under my roof, that I don't even consider myself worthy to come to him." They moved toward the door, but I pulled them back and added, "Tell him to just say the word and my servant will be healed. I know he can do this because I myself am a man under authority, with soldiers under me. I tell one, 'Go,' and he goes; and another one, 'Come,' and he comes. I say, 'Do this,' and my servant does it. Now go!" And they went.

I had heard that with Jesus, there was no hocus pocus, no complicated rituals or magic concoctions. He healed with only a word here and a simple touch there. It was obvious to me, based on my military experience, that Jesus had authority over illness like I had over my troops. If I gave an order, it was obeyed immediately and without question. So I expected Jesus could do the same with illness—from any distance. All he needed to do was give the order and my servant would be made well again. I was convinced of it.

But after it appeared my friends had finished talking with Jesus, he and his followers continued to walk nearer to my house anyway. I was astonished. I felt overwhelmed by my sense of unworthiness. I truly believed I was totally unworthy for the Messiah to come into my house. So I bolted from my servant's bedside, out through the courtyard, and fell at Jesus' feet. I pleaded, "Lord, I do not deserve to have you come under my roof. But just say the word and my servant will be healed." I repeated all that I told my friends to say to him about the authority I had and knew he had too.

And then Jesus told those who followed him something I will never forget. He said, "I tell you the truth, I have not found anyone in Israel with such great faith." I couldn't believe it. Was he really talking about me? How could a Roman soldier have greater faith than a Jew who grew up in the Jewish faith tradition? I came out to give Jesus the honor and respect he was due. But here he was affirming and praising me.

He went on to say that I would be among many non-Jews from every race and culture who would join Abraham, Isaac, and Jacob at the ultimate celebration in heaven. Amazing! It was as though Jesus were an insider, knowing who would be in heaven in the end. It was hard to grasp how I, and other non-Jews, could be counted worthy of sitting at the same table with the forefathers of the Jewish faith.

But the God of Israel must truly be the God of not just Israel, but the God of all peoples, of all the world. And Jesus talked with such authority, as though he knew the heart of God.

Jesus also noted that there will be Jews who will mourn because they will not be included in God's kingdom. I wondered how it could be that there will be non-Jews like me who will get into heaven, and Jews who will not. And how would Jesus know? I now think that it may be that these Jews had assumed their citizenship was a birthright. They didn't see it as an undeserved gift, as I did, given to them because they simply and humbly trusted God. And Jesus could only know who would not get into the kingdom if God had told him. He must have a special relationship with God for him to know something like that.

Jesus finally said to me, "Go! It will be done just as you believed it would." How humbling! The Great Messiah made me, unworthy as I was, feel enormously honored. Without stepping foot inside of my house, he just gave the word, as I asked him to, and granted the desire of my heart. What authority and power! And at the same time, what respect and humility! I know of no one like him.

Immediately, I sent my friends back into the house to care for my servant because I really did believe that Jesus had healed him. Almost as soon as they had entered the cool darkness of my house, one of them came dashing out, yelling, "It's true. He's well! He really is well!" And, after that, to everyone's amazement, out walked my servant, squinting to protect his eyes from the harsh rays of the sun, wobbly and weak from the terrible trauma his paralyzed body had just been through. Sweat still drenched his nightclothes and dripped from his forehead as he recounted to us what he experienced when, in an instant, he was miraculously healed. He was baffled by what happened so we told him how Jesus had given a command that he be healed and it was so. My servant was awestruck, went to Jesus, knelt in reverence before him and poured out his gratitude.

Jesus then told me, "Your servant is very weak. Perhaps if you gave him some food, he would feel better." I had not even considered the needs of my servant. What compassion and mercy Jesus showed. So I told one of my servants, "Go and prepare a meal for your fellow servant who was sick but is now healed. On second thought, why not make something for the whole household and some guests? Let's have a big celebration!" I especially wanted Jesus to stay for the celebration so I could thank him and introduce him to my servant, not only as the person who made him well, but, also and most of all, as the Messiah we were both hoping and praying would come soon.

Although I felt unworthy of Jesus coming under my roof, since he had already come all this way and was practically standing on my doorstep, I also felt it would be extremely inconsiderate and disrespectful of me not to invite him and his followers to join us. So I inched my way up to him, cleared my throat, and said, "As much as I still feel completely unworthy of having you grace my house with your presence, it would be a tremendous honor and privilege to have you and your companions stay and dine with us today." He accepted without hesitation. And together we enjoyed the most joyful celebration I had ever experienced. Imagine, the Messiah, in my home, talking, eating, getting to know us. What a great taste of what it will be like at the never-ending feast in heaven. Praise be to God!

As a result of all of this, my faith that Jesus was indeed the Messiah, the Savior of the Jews, was fully confirmed. But more than that, it dawned on me the meaning of what Jesus had said to his followers earlier about my faith; Jesus was saying that the salvation he brought was not for the Jews alone, but for the entire world, including me. Who but the Messiah could know so much about who would be included in the kingdom of heaven. I had sought healing for my servant and I had received salvation for myself as well.

This, too, was great news for my family. First, many of those who were with me when I had experienced and heard these things responded in faith to Jesus. Then many others who were close to me or among their family and friends also believed. And, to top it all off, I rejoiced in sharing citizenship in God's kingdom, not only with my family and friends, but also with my faithful and now healed servant. Thank God!

However, as much as my household and network of friends benefited from what Jesus said and did that day, the Jewish community in Capernaum did not fare as well. Many of the Jewish elders were actually offended by what Jesus said and how he said it. And, because Capernaum was Jesus' home base, whenever he was in town, he continued to speak in our synagogue about the coming new kingdom, and do even more miracles among the people. But, in spite of the fact that we benefited more from Jesus' presence than any other town, few believed because of the skepticism of our spiritual leaders and the doubt they instilled in our fellow townspeople. I also hate to think that my faith in Jesus and what he said about me might have been a stumbling block that prevented many Jews in Capernaum from embracing Jesus as their Messiah and entering the kingdom of heaven. But, who am I to question what the

Savior said and did on my behalf and that of my servant that day.

All this also had a profound impact upon Jesus' closest followers, including Peter, Andrew, James and John, the two sets of brothers who were partners in the same fishing business before they left Capernaum to follow Jesus. They left town hoping they were following the Jewish Messiah. They returned to town to experience an object lesson that the Messiah they followed was, in fact, far more than that—that he was and is not only the Savior of the Jews, but of all races and cultures, the Savior of the whole world. Amen!

Reflection Questions:

- What did this encounter with Jesus reveal about him that you knew already?

- Did you learn something new about Jesus (his identity, personality, character, appearance, background, values and beliefs) or about the way he related to people? If so, what did you learn, and how do you feel about him now?

- Jesus encountered the following people in this story:
    - Jewish elders
    - Friends of the centurion
    - The centurion
    - The paralyzed/healed servant
    - The centurion's household

    Discuss the following about these people:
    - What was their relationship to one another before they met Jesus?
    - What was their view of Jesus and how did they relate to him?
    - How did Jesus respond to them?
    - Whom did Jesus positively impact, and whom did he negatively impact? What does this say about Jesus?

- What had the centurion been through that prepared him to meet Jesus?

- The Jewish elders seemed to think that the centurion was worthy of Jesus granting his request to heal his servant because he loved the Jewish people and even built their synagogue. Since Jesus went with them, do you think he thought the centurion was worthy of the healing he could give? Why or why not?

Personal Application Starter:

The Roman centurion was used to wielding authority. He commanded approximately one hundred soldiers in Capernaum, home base for Jesus and his followers. Although he was Roman, a member of the occupying force in the predominantly Jewish region, he was also keenly interested in Jewish culture and religion. He was instrumental in helping the Jewish leaders build the local synagogue because he often participated in Sabbath activities there. Such non-Jewish seekers were called "God-fearers." As a result, a number of Jewish leaders were willing to advocate for the centurion when one of his Jewish servants became critically ill. They were willing to do this on his behalf despite the fact that Jesus was well-known in the area and that many viewed him with suspicion. Jesus had often spoken in their synagogue on the Sabbath, taught on the local beaches, and performed amazing miracles in their midst. So, both the centurion and the Jewish leaders were well acquainted with him.

Much of the centurion's interest and involvement in the Jewish community was due to his relationship with his sick Jewish servant. It was extremely unusual for a Roman centurion to request the mediation of Jewish religious spokesmen to ask a radical Jewish religious leader for help. He risked great embarrassment to do so. He cared for this servant to such an extraordinary degree that he was willing to risk rejection and ridicule from his fellow Romans, the soldiers under his command, the Jewish leaders, Jesus and his followers, and the throngs of townspeople who were around wherever Jesus went.

Jesus responded to the centurion's request conveyed by the Jewish leaders and was walking to the centurion's home to heal the sick servant when some friends of the centurion stopped him. One of the centurion's servants had run back to report what had happened and that Jesus was on his way. When the centurion heard that the Jewish leaders had told Jesus he deserved the healing of his servant because of his role in building their synagogue, the centurion sent his friends back because he didn't feel he was worthy to have Jesus come to his home. The centurion recognized Jesus' authority and power by hearing him teach and seeing him heal at the synagogue and elsewhere. The centurion, being a man of authority himself, believed that Jesus did not have to be present to heal his servant. That is why he sent word to Jesus through his friends that he could stop where he was and simply command that his servant be healed and he would be. But Jesus continued to the home of the centurion anyway.

When the centurion saw Jesus approaching, he dashed out to prevent Jesus from coming closer. He didn't feel worthy to have Jesus enter his home, so he said the same thing he had told his friends to tell Jesus. Impressed by the centurion's faith, Jesus told his followers that he had not seen such faith among all the Jews in Israel and that the centurion, together with many other non-Jews of faith from around the world, would be at the final banquet in heaven, while many Jews expecting to be there will not be. Then Jesus gave the word and the centurion's servant was healed.

A celebration followed with Jesus and his disciples as honored guests, and a wave of new faith and deeper relationships swept through the centurion's household on that miraculous day.

Personal Application Questions:

- What impact did the Roman military leader's story have on you, if any? Did it open your eyes or heart to anything new? What, if anything?

- Have you ever been responsible for the well-being of someone close to you? If so, how have you felt about the responsibility? And what have you done or what would you do in the event of a crisis involving the person you're responsible for? If not, how would you feel about having such a responsibility in the future?

- Have you ever felt caught between two races, cultures, or religions? If so, how have you dealt with it? If not, have you ever been in situations where you've had to relate to people of different races, cultures, or religions? How have you fared in those situations?

- Have you ever chosen to associate with a person or group who could jeopardize your job, reputation, or relationships? If so, why did you do it? How did it turn out? Would you do it again? Why or why not? If you've never done it, would you do it under the right circumstances, and what would those circumstances have to be?

- Have you ever had a positive relationship with someone from a different race, religion, or culture? If so, what did you gain from the relationship? If not, why not? And would you be open to having one?

- Jesus seems to have been able to relate well to people of races, religions, and cultures different from his own. How was Jesus able to do that? How do you feel Jesus would relate to you and your race, religion and culture?

- If someone close to you were sick and dying, and you tried everything possible to get help, but nothing worked, what would you do? If Jesus were living in our day and time today, would you go to him for help? Do you think he would want to help you? Do you think he could?

- Do you think Jesus has the kind of authority the Roman military leader thought he had? Why or why not?

- How would you feel if Jesus assured you that, no matter what your race or ethnicity may be, you too have a place in the kingdom of heaven? Would you be encouraged to follow him? Why or why not?

Chapter Four

The Bartimaeus Encounter
Jesus Heals Disability and Brokenness

The Bible:

Mark 10:46-52

Then they came to Jericho. As Jesus and his disciples, together with a large crowd, were leaving the city, a blind man, Bartimaeus (that is, the Son of Timaeus), was sitting by the roadside begging. When he heard that it was Jesus of Nazareth, he began to shout, "Jesus, Son of David, have mercy on me!"

Many rebuked him and told him to be quiet, but he shouted all the more, "Son of David, have mercy on me!"

Jesus stopped and said, "Call him." So they called to the blind man, "Cheer up! On your feet! He's calling you." Throwing his cloak aside, he jumped to his feet and came to Jesus.

"What do you want me to do for you?" Jesus asked him. The blind man said, "Rabbi, I want to see."

"Go," said Jesus, "your faith has healed you." Immediately he received his sight and followed Jesus along the road.

Luke 18:35-43

As Jesus approached Jericho, a blind man was sitting by the roadside begging. When he heard the crowd going by, he asked what was happening. They told him, "Jesus of Nazareth is passing by." He called out, "Jesus, Son of David, have mercy on me!" Those who led the way rebuked him and told him to be quiet, but he shouted all the more, "Son of David, have mercy on me!" Jesus stopped and ordered the man to be brought to him. When he came near, Jesus asked him, "What do you want me to do for you?" "Lord, I want to see," he replied. Jesus said to him, "Receive your sight; your faith has healed you." Immediately he received his sight and followed Jesus, praising God. When all the people saw it, they also praised God.

The Story:

I'm Bartimaeus. From Jericho. Great place to learn about the world if you can't travel. Merchants from all over pass through. Busy place. Grungy, but colorful—we're proud of our history. Ages ago, God did a miracle—right here—made the huge city walls fall down. We Jews tore the rest of the old place apart—but built it back up again, brick by brick—made it what it is today.

Awhile ago, I was "poor, blind" Bartimaeus. Believe it or not, I used to be blind. Couldn't see a darn thing. When you can't see, you can't work. When you can't work, you can't make any money. Wasn't just blind. I was blind and poor!

I wasn't what you'd call "a productive member of society." But I did what I could. I begged. At times—even filled my money bag. Often picked up coins from far off lands. I did my part to make this city great—brought money into the economy!

While some beggars begged near the houses of the rich or went where the locals worked and shopped, I begged at the city gate. Became kind of a celebrity. Everybody knew my name—missed if I wasn't there. I was the first to say "hi" to visitors when they arrived and the last to say "bye" when they left. I was called Jericho's "unofficial, one-man, welcoming committee." I kinda liked that. Made me feel important. Useful.

My favorite thing about begging at the gate was I heard everything—got the news uncensored—the straight dope. Strange thing though—people often yelled at us blind folk. Seemed to think just cuz we're blind, we're deaf too! But I gotta say, my hearing was just fine. In fact, I could hear better than most—nothing to see to distract me—could focus on just what I wanted to hear—and I heard plenty! Who was in town; who wasn't. Who was visiting; where they were staying. Who was getting married; whose marriage was on the rocks. Whose business was booming; whose was going belly up. Who was born; who died. Which new ideas were taking off and which weren't. What's hot; what's not.

Not everyone stopped at the gate to talk—but many did—even young scholars and shrewd businessmen. I was eager to grill them for information. In my younger days, they might have been put off by my badgering. But lately, they put up with me and told me new things they learned. I loved to talk about religion and philosophy cuz I never felt welcome at the synagogue. So I asked all my questions about God—and life—under the open sky by the city gate.

Foreigners seemed friendliest—guess it's cuz they wanted something from me too. Information. They wanted to know all kinds of things—the best place to stay—where to get a good meal—who would be most interested in buying their stuff—and who was honest and fair. And who could they go to get all their questions answered? Anyone could tell them—me, Bartimaeus.

I gave them what they wanted. And they gave me what I wanted. Not just money. But ideas. News. Things about economics, politics, history, and religion. As I said before, I love religion! Couldn't get enough about all the different ones. Strange thing, though. So many fascinating religions. But I kept coming back to one. The one I grew up with. The religion of the Jews.

Our scriptures are so full of stories—stories a simple man like me can relate to—real life stories—stories that actually happened. The boy David killing the giant Goliath with just a stone; Joseph—sold into slavery by his brothers—becoming Pharaoh's right hand man—finally saving his family and our people; Moses parting the Red Sea—leading our people out of Egypt into the Promised Land; Joshua leading our people to conquer Jericho—walls falling down when people shouted and trumpets sounded. The God of Abraham, Isaac, and Jacob—so active—so alive—so involved in the lives of people—real people—my people. Always saving people—saving us.

Then, amazing reports started coming through the gate. What a buzz! I was all ears. A traveling teacher—with insight never heard of before—wisdom to rival Solomon's—teaching with authority—like a prophet of old—not like the Pharisees. Thousands flocking to hear him—powerful—passionate— inspiring. But down-to-earth, approachable—compassionate. From Galilee—Nazareth, but born in Judea—Bethlehem. A carpenter—rabbi—miracle worker—healer.

His name—Jesus. I heard stories of how he fed thousands of people with scraps of food. Brought the dead back to life. Healed people with all kinds of diseases. And—healed paralyzed people, deaf-mutes, and the blind. Yes, the blind! People like me.

I remembered a prophecy by the prophet Isaiah. A savior will come to deliver Israel. And the eyes of the blind will be opened. Ears of the deaf unplugged. The lame will leap like deer. Tongues of the mute will sing. Never before have we heard of anyone who could heal like that. Until now. Could it be?

Later I learned about another prophecy. From the prophet Micah. A ruler in Israel will come from the tribe of Judah. From a little town. Bethlehem—where King David was born. He'll have royal blood—from the line of our greatest king. A Son of David. Jesus was born in Bethlehem! Could it be?

But, reports like this—hard to believe. Heard it all before. Someone claims to be Messiah—gains a quick following. Hopes rise—only to fall again. He turns out to be a fraud, a hypocrite—his rebellion—soon snuffed out by the Romans. But, this time, there's something different about this Jesus.

The crowds and his teachings are one thing. But the bloodline of King David—and even more—the miracles and healings—no ordinary man could do those things—only God working through him. And if he could really heal the blind, maybe someday . . . someday he could heal me. I just had to meet this Jesus for myself—so, I waited and waited for word of his coming.

While I waited, I dreamed of seeing. Dreamed of all I could do if I could see—the person I could be—places I could go. I could go to the synagogue and people would welcome me. I could visit the temple in Jerusalem. I could learn a trade—get a real job—buy a home—find a wife—become a papa—spoil my grandchildren. I could really be somebody!

Finally, Jesus did come to our city. But he got past me somehow. Maybe he came before I got to my spot. Or, maybe I left for a bite to eat or to relieve myself. But, somehow I missed him. I was shocked when I heard he was here—right here in Jericho. How could he have passed me? I dunno, but he did. In any case, Jesus was here in Jericho teaching, healing, doing amazing things—causing rumors to fly. I heard new Jesus stories at the gate every day. He was the biggest show in town!

Then one day, I heard familiar sounds—but this loud, I never heard before. Hundreds of sandals shuffling—robes rustling—coming my way. Dust stung my eyes—dried out my nose—stench of body odor everywhere. It was a huge crowd. But not noisy. Very orderly—apparently, trying to hear someone—someone who was answering their questions.

Could it be? Was it him? Yes! I heard his name—Jesus!

I wanted to cry out—but a voice inside me stopped me. How do you know he really heals? Even if he could, why would he heal you? What makes you so special? Why would he care about you? But another voice within me shot back, "He does care. He can heal—and he will."

All of a sudden, I was yelling, "Jesus, Son of David, have mercy on me!" It came from deep inside of me—out my gut and through my lips. Again I screamed, "Jesus, Son of David, have mercy on me!"

I caused a stir. People scolded me, "Bartimaeus, what are you doing? Be quiet!" But I wouldn't listen. I just knew I had to get his attention. I knew if I did, he would heal me. I knew it was now or never.

I cried out even louder, "Son of David, have mercy on me!"

All of a sudden, the shuffle and rustle stopped. The smell of the crowd surrounded me. It was a hushed silence. I could feel hundreds of eyes staring at me—maybe pitying me—maybe disgusted with me. The crowd stopped at the gate. But, had Jesus moved on and out the gate? More silence—my shoulders drooped—my chin dropped—hope had sunk in my chest. But then, a lone voice rose from the crowd, "Cheer up! On your feet! He's calling you."

My heart skipped a beat. Did I hear what I thought I heard? Could it be true? Was he really calling me? Or, was it someone else? I didn't hear Jesus say anything. But, it had to be him calling me. I just couldn't believe it. I tried to gather myself—wanted to go to him with some dignity. But when I got up, I stumbled. Forget dignity. I threw my cloak aside and began moving toward the voice—waving my arms frantically trying to find my way through the crowd. Helpful hands grabbed my shoulders from behind—guided me 'til I was right in front of him.

Then another hand—a strong hand—grasped my shoulder from the front. "What do you want me to do for you?" Jesus asked. No hint of frustration, pity or sarcasm was in his voice—just a warm, straightforward question. He talked to me like an equal—like a real human being. He respected me. I couldn't believe it. There I was—me—Bartimeaus—poor blind beggar—face-to-face with Jesus—Son of the great King David—who I figured to be the Messiah—and he was asking me what I would like him to do for me—like he was my servant or something. Amazing. I thought of my dreams—what I'd do if I was like everyone else—so, I stuttered, "Rabbi, I want to see." My heart pounded. Then Jesus simply said, "Go, your faith has healed you." And just like that, I could see.

The light was blinding. But my eyes soon got used to it. Then, I saw a man—not much taller than me. Tanned. Lean. Not much to look at really, but, oh, what a beautiful sight—smiling at me!

I looked around. The colors! Green trees. Brown, dusty streets. People wearing red, yellow, blue . . . I walked around. Touched everything. The old gate. The walls of Jericho. The stone well. I was like a kid exploring a new world.

I found my way back to Jesus—in the middle of the crowd. All eyes stared at me—but all I wanted to do was look at Jesus. I looked into his face—the face of one who had the power to heal the blind—the Messiah—no one could ever convince me otherwise. I held his face in my hands. Looked into his eyes. Tears of joy poured down my cheeks. Tears of compassion wet his. I thanked him over and over. Kissed him on each cheek, as we Jews do, out of a thankful heart too full to speak.

Jesus healed me. He simply said, "Go, your faith has healed you." Simple but powerful words. No chanting. No ceremony. No hocus pocus. No stuff put on my eyes. Just a few words. What power!

Jesus told me it was my faith—faith he saw in me—that healed me. I didn't see it—didn't know it was in me. But, when he showed up, I had to decide. Believe and call out to him—or doubt, say nothing, and let him pass by. I was forced to choose. I called out to him. Then he called out the faith in me. I see it now.

But then I started to see more. It wasn't just my physical eyes that were opened—my spiritual eyes were opened as well. My faith, at first, was only enough to call out to him. It got my eyes healed. But my faith was so small—as small as my torn and tattered moneybag. I needed and wanted so much more.

He said I was free to go—but I couldn't. I couldn't just say thank you and leave. Yes, Jesus said "go." But my feet said "no"—they wouldn't let me. Sure, now I could go after all those dreams I had—but instantly—I had new dreams. A new life and a whole new world opened up to me. That new world was Jesus!

After meeting Jesus, I just had to know more about him. He looked so ordinary but was so powerful! God was with him like no one else I had ever met or imagined. He was full of God's power to heal. What kind of a relationship with God did Jesus have so he had the faith to do such miraculous things? I wondered. I figured, if I followed him, maybe I could find out how to have such a relationship with God and more faith. Maybe his faith would rub off on me.

It was glaring to me how unlike me he was. I was a beggar—begged for money—begged for my next meal—even begged for the latest news. I only thought of "me"—what I wanted and needed—what others could give me. But it was obvious—Jesus only thought of others and what he could give them. He taught them—helped them—fed them—healed them. He was such a godly man—so unlike me.

Yet, it continued to amaze me that he didn't look like anything special. In that way, he was like me—ordinary looking. I called him "Son of David," but he didn't look like a king. Not the kind of Messiah I expected. But his power. His care for people. Could someone who heals a blind man like me, save a whole nation? Not sure how—but I was convinced he could. I wanted to find out.

I wanted to know him—not just know about him. I knew a lot about him already based on the stories I heard about him by the city gate. I wanted to really know him—so I could find out what he's like on the inside. Then, maybe he could help me be like him and get what he's got—have faith like his—have a relationship with God like his—become such a godly man like him. Maybe I could fully discover what the Messiah is all about.

So I had a choice. Remain a beggar. Stay wrapped up in what I need. Try to make it on my own. Go my own way. Follow my dreams. OR, I could become someone really different. Get more faith. Care more about others. Become more godly. How? By following Jesus—getting to know him—becoming like him—joining him to save our people.

So I chose. Followed David's Son out of Jericho. Left my gate—left security—left begging behind—forever. Followed Jesus, and couldn't help but praise God. Kept telling people along the way what he did for me. Couldn't stop talking about Jesus. Mercy-giver. Healer. Power to make a blind man see. And many recognized me. Said "you were that blind beggar." Others backed up my story. They said, "That's right, he was always at

Jericho's main gate." And because of this many believed what I said about Jesus. And they praised God too!

New friends. New places to see. New joy of being alive. What more will the Son of David do for me?

Reflection Questions:

- What did this encounter with Jesus reveal about him that you already knew?

- Did you learn something new about Jesus (his identity, personality, character, appearance, background, values and beliefs) or about the way he related to people? If so, what did you learn?

- What had Bartimaeus been through that prepared him to meet Jesus?

- Why did Bartimaeus call Jesus, "Son of David," when he cried out to him? How do you suppose Bartimaeus was able to identify Jesus as the Son of David?

- Jesus told Bartimaeus that it was his faith that healed him of his blindness. Didn't Jesus have the power to heal Bartimaeus of his blindness whether he had faith or not? Why would it be Bartimaeus' faith that would cause his healing? Was it actually Bartimaeus' faith or in whom he had faith that healed him?

- Why did Bartimaeus cry for "mercy" instead of for something like help or healing? Do you think that what he asked for made a difference to Jesus? Why or why not?

- After Bartimaeus was cured of his blindness, Jesus told him to "Go." Instead, Bartimaeus followed Jesus. Why would someone give up the dreams of a lifetime to follow Jesus? What do you think of the choice he made? How do you think Jesus responded to Bartimaeus when he chose to follow him instead of going wherever else he could choose to go?

- Note the impact Bartimaeus had on others when he followed Jesus. Would it have been different if he had followed his own dreams? If so, how would it have been different? If not, why not?

- What do you imagine happened to Bartimaeus after he followed Jesus? What might have happened to him if he had chosen to go his own way?

- Is Bartimaeus someone people today can relate to? Why or why not?

Jesus Heals Disability and Brokenness

Personal Application Starter:

Bartimaeus was a person with a physical disability that limited his opportunities in life. He was blind. In spite of his limitations, he was resourceful enough to find a way to meet his needs; he became not only a beggar, but also a supplier of essential tourist information. He planted himself at the city gate like a visitor information booth. He did not make much money, but by accepting his disability and making the most of his situation, he did not starve, and his life became rather predictable and secure. As stable and similar day-to-day was for Bartimaeus, he also found ways to continue learning and growing as a person. In particular, he was on a spiritual journey. Learning to live with his disability and making the most of his difficult situation didn't mean that he no longer wanted to be freed from his limitations and pursue other things in life. He did. And so, when the only possibility for that to ever happen came his way, he wasn't going to let the opportunity pass by him. He gathered all the faith and courage he could muster, and called out to the only hope he had of ever being healed. He called out to Jesus.

For some time, Bartimaeus had been exploring many religions. He talked to travelers from all over the world. Interestingly, Bartimaeus ended up where he began, believing in the religion of his own people, the Jews. His blindness enabled him to concentrate on what he was learning. He remembered many stories of how God saved his people time and time again. He also remembered the prophecies of a coming Messiah who would ultimately deliver Israel and all its people from all that oppressed them forever. The Jewish scriptures spoke of specific things that the Messiah would do that would enable the Jews to recognize him when he came. And, Bartimaeus had heard the stories, not of old, but new, current stories of how this man named Jesus was doing those very things. This was the reason that Bartimaeus cried out to Jesus that day at the city gate by calling him the Son of David, another way the Messiah was to be recognized. Jesus was, in fact, a descendant of King David.

Bartimaeus cried out for mercy and Jesus heard his cry. Jesus healed Bartimaeus of his blindness and told him that it was his understanding and belief in who he, Jesus, was as the Messiah that enabled him to be healed. Jesus then told Bartimaeus that he was free to go and, in effect, seek to fulfill all the hopes and dreams Bartimaeus had been harboring in his heart all these years. But, in spite of the fact that he was free to go, his feet said "no." Immediately, Bartimaeus realized that he had new hopes and dreams, and they all revolved around Jesus. He wanted to know Jesus better, not just more about him. And, the only way he could do that was to follow him. So, that's just what he did. As a result, his life and relationship with God were transformed, and the lives of many others were dramatically changed as well.

Personal Application Questions:

- What impact did Bartimaeus' story have on you, if any? Did it open your eyes or heart to anything new? What, if anything?

- Do you have any sort of disability, whether physical, mental, emotional, or social, that limits opportunities in your life? If so, what is it? How have you coped with it? Has it made you a stronger or weaker person? If not, how have you treated or felt towards those who do have a disability?

- If you have a disability, have you been able to maintain a positive self-image in spite of what others might think of you or how they might treat you? If so, how have you been able to do so? If not, is there anything you can do about it on your own, or do you need help to overcome your negative self-image? Where would you get help?

- If you don't have a disability, what disability are you most frightened about getting? If you did become disabled with that disability, how do you think you would handle it?

- Are you on a spiritual journey as Bartimaeus was? If so, where are you on that journey? If not, why not? And what would get you going on one? Would you like to have the kind of faith that Bartimaeus had? Why or why not? If so, how would you develop that faith?

- If Jesus healed you of a disability as he did Bartimaeus, what would you do—go and pursue your hopes and dreams, or follow Jesus wherever he might lead, as unpredictable as that might be? Why?

• Do you feel ready to meet and/or get to know Jesus better at this time in your life? Why or why not? How might he change your life and the lives of others around you if you did?

Chapter Five

The Demoniac Encounter

Jesus Overpowers Mental Illness and Spiritual Oppression

The Bible:

Mark 5:1-20

They went across the lake to the region of the Gerasenes. When Jesus got out of the boat, a man with an evil spirit came from the tombs to meet them. This man lived in the tombs, and no one could bind him any more, not even with a chain. For he had often been chained hand and foot, but he tore the chains apart and broke the irons on his feet. No one was strong enough to subdue him. Night and day among the tombs and in the hills he would cry out and cut himself with stones.

When he saw Jesus from a distance, he ran and fell on his knees in front of him. He shouted at the top of his voice, "What do you want with me, Jesus, Son of the Most High God? Swear to God that you won't torture me!" For Jesus had said to him, "Come out of this man, you evil spirit!"

Then Jesus asked him, "What is your name?"

"My name is Legion," he replied, "for we are many." And he begged Jesus again and again not to send them out of the area.

A large herd of pigs was feeding on the nearby hillside. The demons begged Jesus, "Send us among the pigs; allow us to go into them." He gave them permission, and the evil spirits came out and went into the pigs. The herd, about two thousand in number, rushed down the steep bank into the lake and were drowned.

Those tending the pigs ran off and reported this in the town and countryside, and the people went out to see what had happened. When they came to Jesus, they saw the man who had been possessed by the legion of demons, sitting there, dressed and in his right mind; and they were afraid. Those who had seen it told the people what had happened to the demon-possessed man—and told about the pigs as well. Then the people began to plead with Jesus to leave their region.

As Jesus was getting into the boat, the man who had been demon-possessed begged to go with him. Jesus did not let him, but said, "Go home to your family and tell them how much the Lord has done for you, and how he has had mercy on you." So the man went away and began to tell in the Decapolis how much Jesus had done for him. And all the people were amazed.

Luke 8:26-39

They sailed to the region of the Gerasenes, which is across the lake from Galilee. When Jesus stepped ashore, he was met by a demon-possessed man from the town. For a long time this man had not worn clothes or lived in a house, but had lived in the tombs. When he saw Jesus, he cried out and fell at his feet, shouting at the top of his voice, "What do you want with me, Jesus, Son of the Most High God? I beg you, don't torture me!" For Jesus had commanded the evil spirit to come out of the man. Many times it had seized him, and though he was chained hand and foot and kept under guard, he had broken his chains and had been driven by the demon into solitary places.

Jesus asked him, "What is your name?"

"Legion," he replied, because many demons had gone into him. And they begged him repeatedly not to order them to go into the Abyss.

A large herd of pigs was feeding there on the hillside. The demons begged Jesus to let them go into them, and he gave them permission.

When the demons came out of the man, they went into the pigs, and the herd rushed down the steep bank into the lake and was drowned.

When those tending the pigs saw what had happened, they ran off and reported this in the town and countryside, and the people went out to see what had happened. When they came to Jesus, they found the man from whom the demons had gone out, sitting at Jesus' feet, dressed and in his right mind; and they were afraid. Those who had seen it told the people how the demon-possessed man had been cured. Then all the people of the region of the Gerasenes asked Jesus to leave them, because they were overcome with fear. So he got into the boat and left.

The man from whom the demons had gone out begged to go with him, but Jesus sent him away, saying, "Return home and tell how much God has done for you." So the man went away and told all over town how much Jesus had done for him.

The Story:

Jesus was tired. He had been teaching and healing many among the Jews for days. He wanted to get away to rest, reflect and regain his bearings. So, he and his closest followers got into a boat and went to the other side of the Sea of Galilee, a region referred to as the Decapolis, a federation of ten non-Jewish towns and cities. There they could retreat from the Jewish crowds who easily recognized him by going to an area where hardly anyone even heard of him. But, while they were on their way, a storm swept across the lake, swamping the boat. There was no way Jesus' followers could keep the boat from filling with water and eventually sinking if the storm continued to rage on as it did. So, in a panic, they woke Jesus who, amazingly, had been sleeping through it all. He calmly told the wind and waves to stop, and, immediately, the storm stopped. A new fear overwhelmed his followers. They thought they knew who they were following by what they had experienced of him so far. But, this shocked them. They wondered, "If he can command the wind and waters, who is Jesus—really?"

Not long after that they arrived on the other side at what appeared to be a quiet place. It was there that Jesus' followers were in for another shock—an encounter that, once again, would shatter the boundaries of their limited understanding of who it was that they called "Master" and hoped would be the Jewish Messiah. The place that they had unknowingly chosen to land was at the foot of a high, rocky embankment. At its top was a graveyard, a place where people buried their dead. It was especially quiet because there was only one permanent resident living among the tombs. I was that person. Hardly anyone came to visit the tombs unless they absolutely had to because of me.

By the way, you might be asking yourself how I knew about what had happened to Jesus and his followers before they ever even met me. I learned these things only because of what they told me after Jesus released me from my torment. I did not understand much of anything until I found myself sitting at Jesus' feet, hearing from Jesus himself and his followers all the horrible and wonderful things that had just taken place leading up to that point. If you would like, let me share with you what happened and what led up to it.

As I was growing up, I spent most of my time alone. I was always huge for my age, and ugly. Also, I was shy and not very social. I was laughed at for all kinds of things—how I dressed, how I talked, how clumsy I was. Taunting children followed me wherever I went, so I hated to go out into the streets. Adults treated me little better. They stared at me with looks that penetrated deep inside of me and made me feel worthless. It would have been different if I were actually as stupid as they thought me to be. I wouldn't have been aware of how they thought of me. My problem was that I knew how I looked and had the same opinion as they did. I looked like a stupid, good-for-nothing giant. However, I also knew what they didn't, that I was at least as smart as most of the people around me and capable of whatever they could do and more. Yet, there I was, trapped in my body. So, I stayed inside my home, which only reinforced peoples' negative opinions of me. As the days, weeks, months and years passed, my self-imposed imprisonment became more and more of a living hell. My family fed me, clothed me, sheltered and tried to console me. But, as time went on, I became more and more violent, hurtful to myself and to others. I would often cut myself and lash out at those who loved me most with hateful words. Because of this, the relationship I had with my family deteriorated to the point where I was treated more as a beloved pet gone vicious and deranged, rather than a confused and lonely family member. As much as they still loved me, they were ashamed of me. So, most of all, they helped to hide me.

At some point, I just couldn't take it anymore. I ran out of the house. I went crazy—really crazy. I ran out of the village and into the hills, tears running down my face. I was yelling—I don't know what—all I could remember was that I was screaming my lungs out! Finally, an enormous cry bellowed from my mouth, bouncing off the rocks—echoing over and over. Curse after curse exploded out of me. I cursed everything and everyone for making my life a living hell. I even cursed myself—everything about me. And worst of all, I cursed the gods—for allowing me to be born! I begged them to either destroy me, or give me power to pour out vengeance upon all those who ridiculed and rejected me.

And then, something horrible happened. I don't know what came over me—but I was filled with darkness. Something I had never experienced before—a depth of darkness I couldn't escape. I was desperate—confused. Fear swept over me like a huge wave, pushing me under and pinning me to the bottom of an angry sea. I felt like I was drowning in the darkness. I began to shake. I couldn't stop shaking. I fell to my knees, sobbing. My body bent at the waist and I began to bob up and down—without stopping—my forehead hitting the dirt and rocks in front of me over and over again. It seemed like forever that I was there on my knees, sobbing and bobbing, and banging my forehead. Out of control.

When my sobbing finally died down, I ran back to town, desperately seeking anyone's help. But, of course, no one did—

all looked away. Why wouldn't they? I was weeping and screaming, bloody and dirty—the person nobody paid any attention to anyway, except to scoff at or mock. And, of course, I didn't see myself. I only saw the horror in the people's eyes. So, I got even more scared. Anger then rose within me, higher and higher, as I was refused help. I ran, howling through the marketplace, pleading, begging for help—overturning tables and carts along the way. All of sudden, I was tackled from behind. A group of men forced me to the ground. They jumped on me, beating and kicking me. Then I felt something hard hit me on the back of my head, and my body went limp.

My hands and feet were in shackles when I awoke. I kicked and screamed, trying to break free . . . but I couldn't. I got to my feet and hopped after them, trying to bite them. I swung my chains, hoping to hurt them in any way I could. The chains were too strong for me to break, so I finally slumped to the ground exhausted. They put me in a place where I could not escape, and from that point on, a guard was posted at all times to stand watch over me. It was not so much for my protection as it was so I wouldn't hurt anyone else.

After a few days of rest in the gloomy silence of my solitary confinement, the uncontrollable anger and fury swirled up within me once again. All of a sudden, I was completely out of control. I howled out obscenities and cursed the gods for my misery. I cried out for any and all gods to have mercy upon me, and give me strength. And, then, it happened.

A powerful dark force surrounded me and then rushed into me, all the way through to my arms and legs. Super human power surged through my entire body. I broke the chains— shattered the door of my makeshift prison—guards and people scattered. I caught some of the men who beat me and took my anger out on them. They were nearly dead when I left them. Then, I ran from town, a crowd chasing after me until I found myself amidst the quiet of the tombs just outside of town—sanctuary—and what became my new home. There, I fell in the dust, moaning and wailing, until I finally dropped off to sleep, drained of all emotion and strength.

I awoke the next morning to wind whistling through the tombs. Then, I heard voices—lots of voices. I jumped to my feet and turned around and around, but saw no one. I screamed, "Where are you?" A voice louder than the rest answered, "Here, here, inside of you!!" "Who are you?" I cried. "We are many. You can call us Legion because we are like an entire company of Roman soldiers," was the answer. "We will take care of you. You will never have to be alone again. We are the ones who gave you the power to break your chains and free yourself from those awful people. You won't have to be afraid of anyone any more. They will be the ones who are afraid." And they were.

The people in town were haunted by the sounds of my constant moaning echoing off the rocks and stone walls of the nearby tombs. Few dared come to the tombs after that. Whenever they did, an uncontrollable rage burst out of me. I would swear at them, swinging my arms wildly as I ran at them like a madman. My broken chains would whip around and catch some of them as they tried to escape.

Wounded, they would leave, yelling threats and curses at me—warning others never to come to the tombs, unless they absolutely had to. For a long time, only my family would dare come to the tombs, bringing me food and fresh clothing. But, after a while, even my family stopped coming. My madness had reached the point where I could not even recognize my own mother.

After that, I lived alone for what seemed like an eternity. I didn't know how long. All I knew was that it had been years. I ate what the herdsmen fed the pigs that foraged nearby. Sometimes a pig would be killed by a wild animal or simply die. I would drag the dead pig back to the tombs and eat it. I even caught fish, injured from trying to escape fishermen's nets. Sometimes I got sick eating raw meat and fish, but it never killed me. In any case, I survived.

Over time, the voices grew louder. They never shut up. They kept talking and talking. I hardly ever slept. I couldn't think. I couldn't do anything without their constant jabber inside my head. Sometimes I couldn't understand what the voices were talking about. Other times, what they were saying was loud and clear. They said hateful things—twisted things. They'd tell me, "It's not your fault you are so ugly. It's not your fault that you are so big and clumsy. It's not your fault that you couldn't control your own strength. They should have helped you. They should have loved you. They deserved to be punished—to be hated—to be hurt. We love you just the way you are—ugly, big and clumsy, out of control—crazy. Yes, you are crazy. But, so what? We will never leave you!"

Talk, talk, talk—jabber, jabber, jabber—I was going out of my mind. I guess I already was. In any case, it got so all I wanted to do was end it all—to stop the noise in my head. I grabbed sharp rocks, broken pieces of pottery, whatever I could get my hands on, so I could cut myself, beat myself, kill myself. But, somehow, no matter what I tried, I couldn't destroy myself!

It was then that the Jewish leader, Jesus, and his followers landed at the bottom of the steep slope. I was unaware of their arrival, but the voices inside of me somehow knew. They began to moan and groan as if something was tormenting them. They told me not to go to the cliff because there was danger lurking down below. They threatened me, "If you go closer, we will punish you." My curiosity grew stronger the closer I got to the edge of the embankment overlooking the shore. With each step, their warning grew louder. "Don't go any further. You'll be sorry!" But, for the first time, I didn't feel like I had to do what the voices told me. With each step, my will seemed to become stronger. So, I cautiously crept closer to the edge until I was able to see the beached boat, and Jesus and his followers walking towards the steep slope leading up to where I was.

Now, the voices within me really started to panic. They yelled, "That man and those others will reject you like everyone else. He will hurt you and then leave you. Then, where will you be—without anyone—not even us?" But, somehow, the closer I got to Jesus and his followers, the less the voices had control over me.

I started to climb down toward the men. Finally, the voices were actually shrieking, begging me, "Please, don't go any closer. What will we do without you? We need you. Don't you want to help us? We've kept you company and protected you all this time. Aren't you grateful for what we have done for you? Please don't go any closer—for our sake."

My will was now strong enough so I could run to Jesus. I ran to him and collapsed on my knees at his feet. All of a sudden, words came pouring out of my mouth that were not my own. The voices within me began shouting at Jesus. A voice from within, louder than the rest, cried out, "What do you want with me, Jesus, Son of the Most High God? Swear to God that you won't torture me!" This was actually the first time I had heard the name of Jesus, the man who seemed to be leading this group of men unknown to me.

The voice within me said this because Jesus had commanded, "Come out of this man, you evil spirit!" This was so amazing. I didn't have any idea who this man was or anything about him, but the voices knew exactly who he was and what powers he had. They not only knew his name, but also recognized that he was the "Son of the Most High God." How strange it was that the voices that tormented me knew the name of Jesus yet Jesus didn't know the name of the evil spirit within me. Apparently, the presence, authority and power of Jesus extended far beyond where his body was located, while the evil spirits only had power and influence over a relatively small geographic area and a limited number of living beings. So, Jesus asked, "What is your name?" The voice within me sounded very reluctant but was forced to answer. "My name is Legion," the evil spirit replied, "for we are many."

Then the demons within me begged Jesus not to send them out of the area, but to send them into the nearby pigs. It seemed they felt like they had more of a chance of surviving here in this area where we knew nothing of this Most High God rather than to be expelled to where Jesus came from and all the people believed that this Most High God could protect them. So Jesus gave them permission. At that instant, something inside of me ripped into a thousand pieces and rushed out of me. The evil spirits entered the herd of pigs which, immediately, stampeded down the steep bank into the lake and drowned. Those tending the pigs dashed back into town and out into the surrounding countryside to tell everyone what had happened. A crowd followed them back to see for themselves what had taken place and who it was that was responsible for the loss of their pigs.

When the evil spirits left me, I fainted. When I opened my eyes again, Jesus was kneeling over me with his hand on my forehead. Jesus smiled and gently talked to me until I was fully conscious. I was half-naked, bruised and bloody, covered with dirt and sweat. So, Jesus asked some of his followers to help him take me down to the lake for a bath and put some clean clothes on me. Once all this was done, I was invited to join them for the meal they had brought with them. It was strange eating and talking so casually with the man the evil spirits called the "Son of the Most High God." This man had proved to me by the authority he had over the evil spirits that what they said of him must be true. More than that, I was now a whole new person. I was the biggest proof of all. There I was, clean, clothed, in my right mind, having a meaningful conversation and a meal with an ordinary looking man who was the Son of God. That's a miracle only the Son of God could do.

By then, the villagers arrived to see what had happened. At first, they were confused. They expected a far different scene than the one they found. They heard of evil spirits battling a person they called the Son of the Most High God—of thousands of evil spirits being driven out of the mad man from the tombs, swarming like bees into two thousand pigs—those same pigs going crazy and stampeding into the lake and drowning. They expected a deserted, bloody battlefield. But, instead, they found a few ordinary-looking men having a pleasant picnic beside the lake. They had a hard time identifying the difference between us; me, the man who used to be crazy and demon-possessed, Jesus who had power greater than the evil spirits, and Jesus' followers, some of whom were taller and even more ruggedly built than Jesus. As I said, they were confused because nothing was as they had expected it to be.

Then, the townspeople noticed the huge herd of bloated pig carcasses floating, belly up, in the lake. They, at first, became angry because the dead pigs represented a huge loss of income. They asked those who were there who was to blame for their loss. But then, they were afraid. After all, the man who sent the evil spirits into the lost pigs was someone the demons called the "Son of the Most High God," not someone to be taken lightly. So, when the pig-tenders pointed Jesus out, the townspeople did all they could do because they knew that they couldn't control Jesus. They begged him to leave.

Calmly, Jesus got up, asked his followers to gather up their things, and began to leave. As he got into the boat, I ran up to him and pleaded with him to let me go with him. I wanted to learn so much more about him and his Most High God. And, I was so grateful to him that I was willing to follow him anywhere, do anything for him, for the rest of my life. But, Jesus said, "No." He told me to go home and tell my family what the Most High God, out of his mercy, had done for me. My family had not come with the others because the tombs had long since become too painful and shameful a place for them to visit. So, they missed the miracle that transformed me.

I went home. I actually had to introduce myself to my own family. Physically, I was the same. But, in other ways, I had changed so much that even my physical appearance seemed different. They were skeptical at first that my transformation was even possible—or permanent. It took some of the townspeople who were there to relate to them what they had seen and heard among the tombs that day before they would fully believe and eventually trust me. I was still huge and not much to look at, but I had a different spirit about me. People were no longer threatened or repulsed by me, but rather they were actually attracted to me. Because of my size, I found it easy to be helpful in ways where more muscle was needed. It took a long time for my hometown to recover from the loss of all those pigs, but I was able to be part of restoring my community to a degree of financial stability.

Over time, anger over the lost pigs dwindled, and my family and many others in town lost their fear of Jesus. I shared my story over and over with as many people as wanted to listen, not only in my hometown but also throughout the Decapolis. It got to the point where many in the entire region were hoping for the day that Jesus, a Jew, and Son of the Most High God, would come back to our non-Jewish area so we could welcome him, learn from him, and be healed by him.

That's why I am here today, telling you my story. I was out of my mind, out of control, and oppressed by spiritual forces that were destroying me. But Jesus freed me—as you see and hear. I am living proof that Jesus does have the power to heal— even the mentally ill and spiritually oppressed. And, I am here to assure you that Jesus is not just the deliverer of the Jews, but that he came to free all people, of any culture and religious background, of whatever it is that oppresses them and holds them in bondage. People tell me that I am the first non-Jew to proclaim Jesus as the Son of God and Lord to non-Jewish people, meaning all people at any time, everywhere! Praise be to God. I hope you have the opportunity to meet him for yourself, so you can discover for yourself, who he is and how he wants to deliver you from the things that keep you from knowing God!

Reflection Questions:

- What did this encounter with Jesus reveal about him that you knew already?

- Did you learn something new about Jesus (his identity, personality, character, appearance, background, values and beliefs) or about the way he related to people? If so, what did you learn, and how do you feel about him now?

- How is it possible that with just a word, Jesus could make the raging wind and waves perfectly calm? If this really happened, what possible answers could there be to the disciples' question, "Who is Jesus—really?"

- How did Jesus relate to the various people in the story?
  - The demonized man
  - Legion
  - The townspeople and pig-tenders
  - His followers

- What had the demonized man been through that prepared him to meet Jesus and believe in him as the Son of the Most High God?

- What was it that Jesus responded to or that led Jesus to cure the man of his mental illness and spiritual oppression? Faith? Worthiness? Pity? Something else?

- Do you believe that demons existed and were active in Jesus' time? How about today? Why or why not?

- What do you think of how the demons reacted to Jesus' presence, how they treated Jesus when they were face-to-face with him, and how Jesus could just say the word and they would go wherever he sent them?

- How do you think Jesus' followers reacted to what they saw, as Jesus spoke with demons, restored the sanity of a mentally ill, spiritually oppressed man, and dealt with the aftermath of angry pig-tenders and townspeople?

- Why did Jesus allow other people to follow him after he healed them, but not this man? What impact did the man have on others because he went home and did not follow after Jesus?

- Is the demonized man someone people today can relate to? Why or why not?

Personal Application Starter:

The demon-possessed man wasn't always that way. He was an unusually large person who was not very handsome. He was also shy. As a result, he had a difficult time making friends and was ostracized for his appearance and lack of agility. In time, his isolation from family and community made him susceptible to extreme introspection, depression and mental illness. He internalized his anger and bitterness until, one day, he exploded. By cursing the gods—spiritual powers other than God—pleading for their help, and begging for their mercy, he opened himself up to be inhabited and controlled by evil spirits. Once he was demon-possessed, the only option for a cure was spiritual. A higher, more powerful spirit had to assume mastery over the demon-possessed man's life and expel the evil spirits. That's when Jesus arrived on the scene and showed the demon-possessed man mercy.

The demon-possessed man had been living among the tombs for some time. Over that time, the evil spirits within were able to take control of more and more of the man's mind, emotions and will. The spirits would often overpower the man and send him into what appeared to be a self-destructive rage. He would beat himself with rocks until blood oozed from black and blue bruises on every part of his body his arms could reach. Scar tissue contorted his face, making it appear to be that of a monster. The voices of the many spirits which occupied his soul would, all at the same time, add their voices to his own—their voices screaming curses and profanity—his voice crying out in pain, pleading for mercy.

As Jesus and his closest followers approached the shore in their boat at the bottom of the steep embankment, the evil spirits within the demon-possessed man somehow sensed that another spirit greater than they was entering into their territory. They realized this more powerful spirit was within another man, the man in the boat, Jesus. They were terrified. So, they started to threaten the demon-possessed man so he would not go down to the shore to meet the group of men who were then disembarking from the boat. The demon-possessed man barely had enough will power to move his body toward the edge of the cliff so he could see what the spirits told him was danger below. Strangely, he felt something he had not experienced since the evil spirits entered him. His will power seemed to grow stronger with every step toward Jesus and his followers. As the demon-possessed man proceeded to climb down the steep slope and as Jesus and his followers hiked up toward him, the evil spirits' threats were changed into pleas begging the man not to go any further. At that point, the demon-possessed man recognized where the source of his power to go against the will of the evil spirits was coming from, so he ran to Jesus and threw himself at Jesus' feet.

One voice spoke out on behalf of all the evil spirits within the demon-possessed man, calling Jesus by name and referring to him as the Son of the Most High God, begging him not to torture them. Jesus commanded them to come out of the demon-possessed man. The evil spirits who mysteriously were many and one at the same time were named Legion. Legion begged Jesus to send them into a herd of pigs grazing nearby. Jesus granted their request and the pigs went stampeding down into the lake and drowned.

When the townspeople heard reports from those who tended the pigs what had happened, they stormed angrily to the place where the pigs they depended upon for their livelihood were drowned so they could punish the person responsible. However, when they arrived they saw something they had never expected. The man who had been demon-possessed was peacefully sitting with Jesus and his followers, bathed, clothed and in his right mind. They then realized that Jesus was not someone they could control. He, after all, had power over the evil spirits. So, they simply begged Jesus and his followers to leave, which they did.

The man who had been demon-possessed ran after Jesus and asked if he could follow him. But, Jesus told him, "No." He instructed the man to go home and tell his family what God had done for him. He was a miraculously changed man, and those changes led to many more changes, not only in his family, but also throughout his town and the region beyond. The demon-possessed man who was famous for haunting the tombs with his howls was now famous for being the gentle giant who was delivered from evil spirits by Jesus, the Son of the Most High God. As a result, many who were not Jews themselves wanted to meet Jesus in person and be delivered of whatever evil forces controlled them.

Personal Application Questions:

- What impact did the demonized man's story have on you, if any? Did it open your eyes or heart to anything new? What, if anything?

- If you were in the boat with Jesus and saw him making the raging wind and stormy waves perfectly calm with just a word, what would you think? How would you answer the question, "Who is Jesus—really?"

- Have you ever felt ridiculed or rejected for personal characteristics or traits that you have no power to change? If so, what characteristics or traits are they? And how have you dealt with and coped with the ridicule or rejection? Also, how has it affected your outlook on life? If not, how have you treated or felt towards those who have experienced such ridicule and rejection?

- Have you ever had any experience with mental illness or evil spirits? If so, what did you experience? And how have you dealt with and coped with it? If not, how have you treated or felt towards those who have experienced mental illness or been oppressed by evil spirits?

- If you saw Jesus speak with demons who feared him, calmly permit them to go into a herd of pigs, restore the sanity of a mentally ill and spiritually oppressed man, and deal with the aftermath of people who were angry about what he had done, what would you think of him? If you could get to know him, would you want to? Why or why not?

- In the story, the demons who called themselves "Legion" referred to Jesus as "the Son of the Most High God." What things have you seen in the stories you've already heard that would validate such a title? What would it take for you to call him that?

Chapter Six

The Rich Young Ruler Encounter
Jesus is Far More than a Teacher

The Bible:

Matthew 19:16~26

Now a man came up to Jesus and asked, "Teacher, what good thing must I do to get eternal life?"

"Why do you ask me about what is good?" Jesus replied. "There is only One who is good. If you want to enter life, obey the commandments."

"Which ones?" the man inquired. Jesus replied, "'Do not murder, do not commit adultery, do not steal, do not give false testimony, honor your father and mother, and love your neighbor as yourself.'"

"All these I have kept," the young man said. "What do I still lack?"

Jesus answered, "If you want to be perfect, go, sell your possessions and give to the poor, and you will have treasure in heaven. Then come, follow me."

When the young man heard this, he went away sad, because he had great wealth.

Then Jesus said to his disciples, "I tell you the truth, it is hard for a rich man to enter the kingdom of heaven. Again I tell you, it is easier for a camel to go through the eye of a needle than for a rich man to enter the kingdom of God."

When the disciples heard this, they were greatly astonished and asked, "Who then can be saved?" Jesus looked at them and said, "With man this is impossible, but with God all things are possible."

Mark 10:17-31

As Jesus started on his way, a man ran up to him and fell on his knees before him. "Good teacher," he asked, "what must I do to inherit eternal life?"

"Why do you call me good?" Jesus answered. "No one is good—except God alone. You know the commandments: 'Do not murder, do not commit adultery, do not steal, do not give false testimony, do not defraud, honor your father and mother.'"

"Teacher," he declared, "all these I have kept since I was a boy."

Jesus looked at him and loved him. "One thing you lack," he said. "Go, sell everything you have and give to the poor, and you will have treasure in heaven. Then come, follow me."

At this the man's face fell. He went away sad, because he had great wealth.

Jesus looked around and said to his disciples, "How hard it is for the rich to enter the kingdom of God!"

The disciples were amazed at his words. But Jesus said again, "Children, how hard it is to enter the kingdom of God! It is easier for a camel to go through the eye of a needle than for a rich man to enter the kingdom of God."

The disciples were even more amazed and said to each other, "Who then can be saved?" Jesus looked at them and said, "With man this is impossible, but not with God; all things are possible with God."

Peter said to him, "We have left everything to follow you!"

"I tell you the truth," Jesus replied, "no one who has left home or brothers or sisters or mother or father or children or fields for me and the gospel will fail to receive a hundred times as much in this present age (home, brothers, sisters, mothers, children and fields—and with them persecutions) and in the age to come, eternal life. But many who are first will be last, and the last first."

Luke 18:18-30

A certain ruler asked him, "Good teacher, what must I do to inherit eternal life?"

"Why do you call me good?" Jesus answered. "No one is good—except God alone. You know the commandments: 'Do not commit adultery, do not murder, do not steal, do not give false testimony, honor your father and mother.'"

"All these I have kept since I was a boy," he said.

When Jesus heard this, he said to him, "You still lack one thing. Sell everything you have and give to the poor, and you will have treasure in heaven. Then come, follow me."

When he heard this, he became very sad, because he was a man of great wealth. Jesus looked at him and said, "How hard it is for the rich to enter the kingdom of God! Indeed, it is easier for a camel to go through the eye of a needle than for a rich man to enter the kingdom of God."

Those who heard this asked, "Who then can be saved?" Jesus replied, "What is impossible with men is possible with

God." Peter said to him, "We have left all we had to follow you!"

"I tell you the truth," Jesus said to them, "no one who has left home or wife or brothers or parents or children for the sake of the kingdom of God will fail to receive many times as much in this age and, in the age to come, eternal life."

The Story:

I was a ruler in our town—one of the youngest ever. I was a member of the town council entrusted with the responsibility of governing our community and resolving disputes. I was someone all the parents urged their sons to be like. I was a good Jewish boy who played by all the rules and was rewarded for it. By being honest, working hard and doing everything that my people and religion expected of me, I had earned the respect and trust of many in my town. I became successful in business, a leader in the community, and admired in the synagogue. Many parents sought to arrange marriages with my parents between their daughters and me.

As I grew up, I never missed going to the synagogue on Sabbath. I was also diligent in my religious education. I had seriously thought of becoming a rabbi, but my parents felt I was better suited for business. However, I continued to be intrigued by the Hebrew Scriptures—the poems, songs, prayers, history and laws. Since, as a youth, I wanted to become a rabbi, I had even begun to memorize all the Scriptures from beginning to end, word for word. I was extremely careful to observe all the laws and regulations I found there, especially the Ten Commandments as given to Moses on Mount Sinai. These ten laws were so important and foundational to our religion that Jewish religious scholars, for generations, have interpreted and debated the true meaning of each one of them in minute detail. I have considered the Ten Commandments the foundation of my life, and have sought to obey each of them as much as is humanly possible. I am a perfectionist, so I believe I have been as faithful to observing the Ten Commandments as anyone could be.

One day, I had heard Jesus teach in the synagogue. He was not a particularly dynamic speaker, as he was someone who spoke with quiet confidence and what seemed to be absolute authority. He didn't debate or interpret the Scriptures. It was as if he was the author himself—God speaking in the flesh. He corrected misinterpretations and explained God's true intent behind the Scriptures. While Jesus was speaking, I peered around the room and noticed the looks on the faces of our Jewish elders and scholars. There was a mixture of awe, fear, jealousy, frustration and anger. They clearly didn't know how to respond to Jesus, the plainly-dressed, carpenter's son, from the backwater town of Nazareth, who had no formal religious training.

After Jesus spoke that Sabbath at the synagogue, he stayed awhile to discuss whatever anyone had difficulty agreeing with or understanding. But after the objections and questions died down, Jesus and his followers left quickly. More than those who simply wanted to converse with Jesus were throngs of additional people inside the synagogue who wanted him to heal them or someone they loved. And many others wanted to see, touch, or meet the person that they had heard so much about— rumors of his teachings, of his miracles, of growing expectations that he might be the leader who delivers us Jews from Roman occupation and oppression. I, too, wanted to speak with him. I, too, was impressed with Jesus and the way he quietly, yet forcefully, spoke of the things of God. I had pretty much everything that could be hoped for in this life, and I wanted to make sure that I would receive everything I expected in the next. So, when Jesus and his followers left the synagogue, I sought to catch up with them so I could ask Jesus what was urgently on my mind. Because his popularity was growing with each day, I was concerned I might not ever have as good an opportunity to speak with him. I knew I had to be aggressive if it was going to be possible. And, it was not so easy.

People were crowding the exit door as if they were trying to escape a house fire. They were packed shoulder to shoulder, pushing and shoving one another, in an effort to be one of the first out the door so they could get close to Jesus and get his attention. So, there I was behind a wall of humanity, blocking me from fulfilling my mission. I avoided the congestion at the door by finding another exit on the other side of the synagogue. I ran around the synagogue and ahead of the crowd as they emerged out into the street in an attempt to catch up to Jesus and his followers who were walking rapidly on ahead. Amazingly, I ran like I had never run before or since, and I was able to get ahead of Jesus and his followers. Thus, I approached him from the opposite direction he and the crowds were traveling.

I ran as quickly as I could and knelt at his feet so I wouldn't miss my opportunity. Actually, I was so anxious that I blurted out my question on the way down before a knee even touched the ground. I said, "Good Teacher, what good thing shall I do that I may inherit eternal life?"

I was stunned by how Jesus responded. He answered my question with his own. He asked me, "Why do you call me good? No one is good but One, that is, God." I don't think he really expected me to answer his question, but rather, I believe, that Jesus knew I hadn't given much thought to calling him "good." I was just being respectful and polite. Jesus, on the other hand, seemed not to have the time for niceties, and wanted to talk about what really mattered as soon as possible. Jesus immediately set the standard for what is truly good by

Jesus is Far More than a Teacher

telling me that only God is perfectly, thoroughly and consistently good. In other words, there is no one in this world who is good if God is our measure of goodness.

What Jesus said made me insecure right from the beginning. I thought I was pretty good, and I was not the only one. Everyone around me—those in the community, at the synagogue, my business associates, my friends and even my family thought of me as a good guy. I was sure of it. My parents couldn't be prouder of me. I hadn't done anything to intentionally hurt or offend anyone—ever—at least as far as I knew. That's why I had asked Jesus if there was some "good thing" I should do to inherit eternal life. I thought of myself as basically a good person who had done a lot of good things for others, and was simply asking Jesus whether there was anything else I needed to do to be worthy of entering heaven. However if, according to Jesus, only God is good, then where did that leave me? At that point, I wondered if I really wanted to hear Jesus' answer to my question. If what he said was true, then I didn't know if there was anything I had done or could do that would enable me to inherit eternal life. I was totally bewildered!

But then, Jesus said that I could enter eternal life if I kept the commandments. When he said that, I was relieved because I had been careful to observe them all my entire life. So, I asked him, "Which ones?" He listed some of them. The commandments Jesus recited were those having to do with how we treat other people. I reflected upon my past. I hadn't murdered anyone, committed adultery, stolen anything, testified falsely, or committed fraud. And, I had honored my parents, and been good to my neighbors. So, at least, according to the commandments Jesus named, I felt like I was in pretty good shape.

Excitedly, I told Jesus I had done all these things ever since I was a child. But, I also knew that there were other commandments given by God to Moses. So I asked Jesus, knowing better than to call him "good" this time, if there was anything else I needed to do.

Before responding, Jesus looked at me with a smile—not just on his lips, but also in his eyes. He reached over with both arms, grabbed both my shoulders and then gently and affectionately shook me back and forth. He was obviously pleased with me. Then, with a big grin and a pleasant chuckle in his voice, Jesus told me that there was something else I needed to do if I wanted to be perfect. The tone of his voice then went from light-hearted to serious. At that point, I kind of expected that Jesus was going to quote the rest of the Ten Commandments—those dealing with our relationship to God. But, instead he told me to go home, sell all I own, give whatever I was paid for my possessions to the poor, return, and follow him. I was shocked! I didn't know what to say or do. I sank from my knees to my seat. I just sat there in the dust, still as a tree stump for a moment—stunned.

As I said, I was a perfectionist. I had strived my entire life to live as good and perfect a life as I possibly could. I sought to be thoroughly ethical. I was honest and fair with everyone. I worked hard at obeying all the rules and regulations of my religion. And, in the process, I earned a good living and an excellent reputation. I believed I had done a lot of good, not only for my family and myself, but for many other people as well. I didn't think I had anything to be ashamed of. In fact, I was proud of the man I had become. I was secure in the conviction that God had rewarded me with wealth in this life for the good I had done and the good person I had become. So, when I went to Jesus, knelt at this feet, and asked him what I must do to inherit eternal life, I was hoping, and, to be honest, I was half expecting that Jesus was going to tell me that I had done all I needed to do—and, in fact, had done more—that I was exemplary, someone others should follow if they, too, wanted to receive God's reward in the next life. But when he said I still lacked something, I was blindsided. I didn't know what to do or think. What motivated me my entire life to live a good life was called into question. Why wouldn't living a good life be enough to inherit eternal life?

I had come to Jesus with what I thought was a simple, straightforward question that I hoped he would respond to with quick affirmation and assurance. Instead, I ended up with many more questions than I started with. These new questions shook the very foundations of my life. I was confused and insecure. My life would never be business as usual ever again until I found out and understood more about Jesus and what he said I lacked to enter heaven. I could not be comfortable. Yes, I had to find out answers to my questions some way, and I still do. But, I wasn't ready to leave everything that day to find out—so I left Jesus and his adoring crowds, confused and sorrowful.

After days passed, I finally gained some composure. I was able to be a bit less emotional about what Jesus had told me and reflect to see if there was any truth to what he said—about what I lacked, and what he said I needed to do in order to enter heaven.

At the beginning of our conversation, Jesus had said that I could inherit eternal life if I obeyed the commandments. He then quoted the commandments dealing with our relationships with people. After I had told Jesus I had obeyed all those commandments, Jesus said that there was something more I had to do to enter heaven. At the time, that was all right with me because, as I believe now, I expected he meant obeying the other commandments among the Ten Commandments related to having a right relationship with God. I knew and had made every effort to obey all those commandments as well. But instead of what I expected to hear next, Jesus told me to leave everything I had spent my entire life to attain—family, wealth, influence, a good reputation, and security—and then follow him. That threw me completely off guard. I couldn't figure out if Jesus had assumed that I had obeyed all the commandments and added one more commandment of his own that would insure my ability to inherit eternal life—letting go of everything and following him—or, by doing so, the commandments dealing with our relationship with God would be fulfilled. However, in either case, I came to the realization as to why this was so upsetting to me. This put a completely new slant on the Ten Commandments—that he, Jesus himself, and following him, was the only sure way of inheriting eternal life.

When it dawned on me, as I was tossing and turning in the middle of the night, what Jesus was actually implying by what he told me I must do to inherit eternal life, I screamed in the darkness of my own bedroom, "What right have you, Jesus, to reinterpret the Ten Commandments in this way? The only way you could possibly have the right and authority to do so would be if you are God himself in the flesh!" The screeching sound of my own voice fully awoke me. I asked myself, "Did Jesus actually believe himself to be God? Perhaps that's why he asked me the reason I called him "good." He was asking me whether I called him "good" because I recognized him as only a teacher or whether I recognized him as God. Obviously, I only went to him because I thought of him as a good teacher, and not God. That's why I didn't even fully understand his question.

But, let's be reasonable. If I knew for sure that Jesus was God, of course I would have followed him. But, I didn't even understand at that time what he was implying about himself—that he was God. If Jesus is God then what he said I must do to enter heaven made perfect sense—if I wanted to enter heaven, I would have to leave everything I had on this earth so I could follow him there. But I didn't catch what Jesus was implying—that he was God—and there was no way I could have been certain enough at that point that he was God for me to be willing to follow him. I would have had to have known far more about him, and, actually, known him far more to ever seriously consider it. And, besides, at that time it would have seemed to me to be an absolutely absurd notion—that the man standing before me, Jesus, was actually God. I could not have imagined how a human being walking on this earth could ever be the infinite, all-powerful, Creator of the universe. Anyway, at that moment, I wasn't ready to give up everything I had spent my entire life to gain, only to lose it all following someone I knew so little about. So, naturally, I didn't follow him. I was no fool.

But, what if, beyond all human reason, it was actually true? That Jesus was, in fact, God? What then? What opportunity did I miss out on? I passed up an invitation by God himself to be his close follower—to find out first hand anything and everything I would ever want to know about heaven and earth—past, present, and future—and, more amazing still, I could actually know God intimately. That would be a matchless privilege beyond description.

In the end, I decided, ironically, I had too much to lose if I wrote Jesus off as just a wonderful fool. I decided to seriously consider what Jesus implied about himself—that, as unreasonable as it might seem, I would pursue getting to know more about Jesus to the point where I was absolutely sure, one way or the other, whether or not Jesus was God. So, I set out to watch and listen from a distance, and, if I became more and more sure of who he was and that he was God or, at least, God's messenger, I would shorten that distance until I could fully make the commitment he required of me to enter heaven. Only then would I become a fully committed follower of Jesus. I am on a journey to get to know Jesus, and curious to know where that journey will eventually lead.

Perhaps, you would like to come along, too. Would you like to join me?

Reflection Questions:

- What did this encounter with Jesus reveal about him that you knew already?

- Did you learn something new about Jesus (his identity, personality, character, appearance, background, values and beliefs)? If so, what did you learn?

- How did Jesus relate to the rich young ruler? Did you find anything about their interaction interesting or worth noting?

- When the rich young ruler decided not to give up all he owned and follow Jesus, what impact do you imagine his response to Jesus had on those around who were aware of their conversation?
    - Jesus' followers
    - The Jewish elders and scholars
    - People who were at the synagogue that day

- When Jesus told the rich young ruler what he'd have to do to inherit eternal life, was he prescribing what everyone had to do or was Jesus addressing this requirement specifically to the rich young ruler? Did Jesus require everyone who wanted to follow him and inherit eternal life to sell all they owned? Or, did Jesus require different things from different people? Why or why not?

- To "follow Jesus" in Jesus' time meant literally to follow him around wherever he went, as well as to be under his authority, to learn to live as he does from his teaching and his life, and to be in life-on-life, constant, close, life-transforming contact with him. How does this path to eternal life differ from the path of obedience-to-the-rules that the rich young ruler was on?

- Why did Jesus only mention the second half of the Ten Commandments, which deals with our relationships with other people, and fail to mention the first half, which deals with our relationship with God? Isn't the first half at least as important, if not more important than the second half? Instead, Jesus talked about following him. Is there a connection between following Jesus and obeying the first half of the Ten Commandments? What, if any?

- In another time and place Jesus said the following to the Jewish leaders: "You diligently study the Scriptures because you think that by them you possess eternal life. These are the Scriptures that testify about me, yet you refuse to come to me to have life." (John 5:39-40) How might this teaching of Jesus relate to the rich young ruler's situation? And what is Jesus saying about himself? What do you think about what he's saying?

- What impact do you imagine the rich young ruler had on the people in his life and around him following his encounter with Jesus?

- Is there any hope for the rich young ruler? Will he ever inherit eternal life? What do you think the future holds for him?

- Is the rich young ruler someone people today can relate to? Why or why not?

Personal Application Starter:

The rich young ruler seemed to have it all together. In the eyes of everyone around him, including himself, he was a good guy. He was not only good, he was very religious. If anyone believed he should get into heaven, it was the rich young ruler.

The rich young ruler wanted affirmation and assurance that he was on the right track, so he asked Jesus if there was anything else he needed to do to inherit eternal life. He was shocked when Jesus told him that he did lack something. To enter into eternal life, Jesus told the rich young ruler, he would have to sell all he owned, give the proceeds to the poor, and follow him.

The rich young ruler was stunned. He had thought that God had rewarded him with wealth and influence for living a good and religious life. He wondered why God would then require him to give up everything he had spent a lifetime to gain to receive God's reward in heaven. The rich young ruler questioned what gave Jesus the right to change what he had always believed was necessary to receive eternal life unless he was God. He didn't know and trust Jesus enough to risk everything he had for what only *might* be, so he went away sad.

But, the rich young ruler continued to wrestle with Jesus' instructions and what he implied about himself—that he was God. Jesus and his invitation to follow him were compelling even though humanly absurd. So, the rich young ruler set out to get to know Jesus better. He would watch and listen until he was sure who Jesus was. If he discovered Jesus to be God, giving up all he valued in exchange for a deeply personal relationship with God by following Jesus would then be a much easier, though nonetheless life-altering, decision to make.

Personal Application Questions:

- What impact did the rich young ruler's story have on you, if any? Did it open your eyes or heart to anything new? What, if anything?

- Do you believe, as did the rich young ruler, that living a good life should qualify you to inherit eternal life? Why or why not?

- Would you be disappointed, as the rich young ruler was, that there was something you lacked in order to inherit eternal life? What would you do if you really did lack something? How far would you go to supply what you lacked?

- Jesus asked the rich young ruler to sell everything he owned and give all the proceeds to the poor so that he could inherit eternal life. Would Jesus ask you to do the same, or something else, to inherit eternal life? If "something else," what would it be and why?

- If you were living during Jesus' time, and Jesus told you that you'd have to follow him—that is, leave everything and go wherever he goes—in order to inherit eternal life, would you do it? Why or why not? If he told you today to "follow" him in order to inherit eternal life, what would you suppose you'd have to do? Would you do it? Why or why not?

- Do you agree with the rich young ruler that Jesus had no right to reinterpret the Ten Commandments in the way he did, except if he were God himself in the flesh? Why or why not? Do you think Jesus believed himself to be God, or the "Son of the Most High God?" What would you think of him if he did?

- How might others around you be impacted, negatively or positively, by your attempts at developing a relationship with God through Jesus? How might others around you be impacted, negatively or positively, by your indifference toward, or rejection of, Jesus and what he teaches?

- At the end of the story, the rich young ruler decided to watch and listen to Jesus at a distance so that he could determine whether or not Jesus was God. He invited you to join him. Do you sense God's presence and guidance as to what you should do now? What response will you give to the invitation?

Jesus is Far More than a Teacher

Iwa

P.O. Box 3796
Gardena, CA 90247-7496
(626)398-3468
email: iwarock@aol.com
www.iwarock.org

To obtain information about Iwa, *The GodMan Series*, *The GodMan Collection*, or the many other resources offered by Iwa, to find out how to order additional copies of *Meeting Jesus: Face-to-Face with God*, or to donate to Iwa, please go to www.iwarock.org or contact Iwa.

www.ingramcontent.com/pod-product-compliance
Lightning Source LLC
Chambersburg PA
CBHW070811050426
42452CB00011B/1989